AN APPOINTMENT WITH GOD

The Feasts of the Lord

Leviticus 23

A Biblical Theology

Robert R. Congdon

CROSSBOOKS
PUBLISHING

CrossBooks™
1663 Liberty Drive
Bloomington, IN 47403
www.crossbooks.com
Phone: 1-866-879-0502

First published by CrossBooks 12/11/2009

ISBN: 978-1-6150-7072-5 (sc)

Library Congress of Control Number: 2009940818

*Unless otherwise indicated, Scripture quotations are from the King James
Authorized Version of the Bible. Copyright © 1987-2005 Online Bible
Edition version 2.00, Jan. 19, 2005. Winterbourne, ON. Canada.*

*The use of other translations does not necessarily represent an endorsement
of that translation, rather, it reflects an updated or literal translation of the
Hebrew or Greek word(s) which the author feels would help in the reader's
understanding and was best phrased by that particular translation.*

*The use of quotes from various authors does not necessarily represent an endorsement
of their theology. It merely represents recognition of their correct conclusion drawn
from the Scriptures in the instance quoted. That is, they have said what the authors
would say, but they said it first, and therefore deserve the annotation.*

Cover & artwork: Brian C. Johnson

*Printed in the United States of America
Bloomington, Indiana*

This book is printed on acid-free paper.

TABLE OF CONTENTS

INDEX TO FIGURES

INTRODUCTION

For the invisible things of Him from the creation of the world are clearly seen . . . Even His eternal power and God head; so that they are without excuse . . .

Romans 1:20

The past intrigues man and the future fascinates him. He feels the same interest in his personal life as well as that of the world around him. The seventy years of a man's earthly life represent but a dot in world history. In terms of eternity, the years of his life shrink to nothingness. Yet the events of his life are extremely important to him. Birthdays, graduations, first job, marriage, the birth of children and grandchildren, along with many other unique events highlight a man's personal moment in history.

In the spiritual realm the highlights may be few or many. For the Christian, salvation marks the high-point of his earthly life. If we sum the individual spiritual events together, a "portrait" of that Christian's life begins to emerge. Some years ago my wife found a number of letters written by her great-grandmother whom she never had met. By reading the letters, she came to know her long-dead great-grandmother through the personality which radiated from the pages.

In a similar way, God left letters to man in order that he might learn of His personality. Through God's interaction with men throughout history, recorded in the Bible, He painted a self-portrait of Himself. We must recognize, however, that finite man can only comprehend the infinite God to a limited extent. God must therefore reach down to man and reveal Himself in ways that man can understand.

God has done this through various mediums of expression. First and foremost, God uses His written revelation, the Bible, to reveal Himself to mankind. He also uses His Creation (Romans 1:20). His interaction with the nation of Israel makes up a third medium of revelation. Finally, He interacts with people on an individual basis throughout the course of their lives. The height of this interaction comes at the time of personal salvation. By examining all of these forms of revelation, man develops a picture of the true and living God's character.

As man successfully pictures God, he brings Him glory and praise. The success of such an endeavor lies in the reliability of his facts and in the quality of his scholarship. Based upon his presuppositions, man attributes creation either to God or to mere chance. False ideas of God often lead to a misinterpretation of salvation truth (Proverbs 14:12). Only God can give man "true truth." Thus, we must rely solely upon the Bible as the clearest and most direct revelation of God. The events recorded in the Bible often clearly reveal God's personality. Unfortunately, in some spiritual areas, man's eyesight is too weak to perceive even the simplest of revelations. Out of His mercy to finite man, God often uses physical comparisons to clarify the things man cannot understand with his own limited understanding.

God creates just such a physical comparison through the nation of Israel and its history. Before the foundation of the world, God planed seven specific interactions with Israel that would serve to illuminate a number of significant truths regarding His dealings with mankind. This collection includes truths which apply to Israel, truths which apply to the Church, and truths which apply to both. In order to make the seven interactions clear to limited human understanding, God created the seven feasts of Israel, described in Leviticus 23, as visual examples. Although both the interactions and the feasts are literal, historical events, the feasts serve double duty when they act as symbols of the interactions.

These seven interactions should be thought of as **appointments** since God designated a specific time, place, and participant for each event. Only God could use such simple pictures--seven appointments--to teach some of the most profound truths in the universe. Only God, Who is all knowing and all powerful, could bring these appointments with Israel to fruition. Examined carefully, the seven feasts which represent the seven appointments serve to reveal three significant areas of truth.

- First of all, the seven appointments act as seven "mountain-top" events in the history of the nation of Israel occurring over many years of time. The seven yearly feasts of Israel picture these seven spiritual appointments. Each feast, therefore, either memorializes a past appointment or prefigures a future one. To date, God has completed four of the seven appointments. Three still await their fulfillment in the future.

- Second, the seven feasts help us to understand the spiritual aspects of salvation and its progressive effects upon us. Israel's interactions with God paint a picture of a man's spiritual journey which begins at the point of salvation and progresses through his life. The seven feasts therefore serve to signify seven steps in the complete salvation process.

- Third, the seven appointments act as seven signposts on the road of time. These landmarks tell us where we are in God's plan for the ages. The seventh appointment will signal the close of history as we know it as well as the beginning of eternity. The first appointment occurred in Egypt at the Feast of Passover. The last appointment will occur in Jerusalem at the Feast of Tabernacles and the Great Jubilee.

For the Jewish people, the feasts serve as yearly reminders of God's tender care for His chosen people. For the Christian, the feasts picture where we are in God's eternal plan. Andrew Bonar states:

It is beautifully supposed by some, that Israel's feasts represent the Course of Time - this earth's days, from creation down to the final end. The Lamb slain [Passover] commences it, and the eighth day of the happy Feast of Tabernacles is its close; while the Sabbath, the rest - God's rest in himself, and his creatures' rest around him - both precedes and follows this Course of Time (Bonar 387).

For the individual, Jew or Gentile, the feasts picture events in his spiritual journey and help him prepare to meet the Author, his Creator.

While individuals earnestly crave to meet God in their own way, one only can meet God as the inerrant and inspired Bible and His Son, the Lord Jesus Christ reveal Him. To see Christ is to see God "*He that hath seen me hath seen the Father…*" (John 14:9). Unfortunately, man often rejects the true picture of God for a god of his own making (Romans 1:16-25). It is the author's hope that you, the reader, will meet the God of the Feasts in the same way that Israel will meet their Lord and see Him face to face at the seventh feast, the Feast of Tabernacles.

The Feast of the Lord	Prime Scripture Reference
Feast of Passover	Leviticus 23:5
Feast of Unleavened Bread	Leviticus 23:6-8
Feast of First Fruits	Leviticus 23:9-14
Feast of Pentecost	Leviticus 23:15-22
Feast of Trumpets	Leviticus 23:23-25
Day of Atonement	Leviticus 16; Leviticus 23:26-32
Feast of Booths	Leviticus 23:33-44
Jubilee	Leviticus 25

Figure 1 – The Feasts of the Lord

CHAPTER 1:
WHAT IS A FEAST?

*To every thing there is a season, and a time to every purpose under
the heaven:*

Ecclesiastes 3:1

The Preacher of Ecclesiastes tells us of an appointed time for every
event in life including birth, death, planting, harvesting, weeping,
laughing, mourning, and dancing (3:2-4). In Leviticus 23 God appoints
seven "*Feasts of the LORD*," significant times for God's people to gather
together for special national events. Before we can look at these times,
however, we must first answer the question, "What is a Biblical feast?"

What is a Biblical Feast?

When you see the word "feast," what picture comes into your mind?
Most people think of a time of eating, usually a holiday. I always think
of Thanksgiving since I truly enjoy this holiday. The family comes
together and celebrates by eating a large meal of turkey, mashed potatoes,
corn, rolls, and pie. This meal reminds us of God's generous care for us
during the past year. Unlike the modern, secularized Christmas with all
of its commercialism, Thanksgiving allows us to focus our attention on
God (or at least it should). For this reason, Thanksgiving shares many
similarities with Biblical feasts. According to the Bible, feasts gather the
people of Israel together for spiritual purposes.

Although Thanksgiving shares many similarities with Biblical
feasts, it is not a perfect match. Some of the feasts described in the
Bible do not involve meals or eating of any kind. Furthermore, some
feasts are actually very serious, somber occasions which may even be

quite painful to the participants. For this reason, I also think of Biblical feasts as a dental appointment.

Every time I go to the dentist, it hurts! Even a simple check-up involves probing and some pain. A dental appointment always involves a set time and place for me to meet with the dentist; in a sense it is a "time to gather." While I am being semi-humorous, a dental appointment is a very serious matter. An important concept emerges from this analogy: a feast is very serious appointment between God and man.

By combining the ideas of Thanksgiving and a dental appointment, we form a picture of the nature of Biblical feasts. Feasts include the following qualities:

- **A gathering together of the nation of Israel**
- **A spiritual meeting with God**
- **An appointed day, time, and place specified by God**
- **Sometimes a joyful time and sometimes a painful one**

As recorded in the Scriptures, God commanded Israel to observe seven feasts throughout the year. Some feasts *do* involve food and a time of thanksgiving. These include the Feasts of Passover and Tabernacles. The Day of Atonement, on the other hand, is a very serious time and even is a fearful time. Other feasts combine seriousness with joy.

A Biblical feast by its very origin and nature involves a spiritual gathering of the nation of Israel. Many students of the Bible have fallen into serious interpretational errors by failing to recognize the fact that the Feasts of the LORD focus uniquely upon Israel and *not* upon the Church. The Church, consisting of all true Believers in Jesus Christ from Acts 2 to the Rapture, never participates directly in the Feasts. The seven appointments, made by God with the nation of Israel, require the direct presence of the nation as a whole. Without Israel, the Feasts cannot exist nor can they be celebrated properly.

In Leviticus 23, God gives the instructions for the seven Feasts of the LORD. This chapter contains the essential details of the Feasts. Other passages throughout the Bible augment our understanding by providing additional information and instructions. Of Leviticus 23, it has been said that no passage of Scripture

... is more doctrinally and prophetically profound and fraught with more of the weight of God's plan for holy living, than the twenty-third chapter of Leviticus. Here is an orderly unfolding of the prophetic panorama, reserved in clarity for the student who will take the time to study it carefully. Here the student will see the prophetic and practical import unfold in progressive and harmonious array. (Strauss 8)

God begins His instructions by addressing the *"children of Israel."* He tells them that the Feasts are *"holy convocations"* for Israel (Leviticus 23:2-3). For this reason He commands the people of Israel to come together for a holy gathering. In order to meet with their Creator and the Sustainer of their nation, they must attend the Feasts. The unique terminology employed in this passage suggests that the command takes the form of a royal decree; the nation therefore has no choice but to meet with its God at these appointments. Clearly, God attaches great importance to these meetings between Himself and His people.

Three Biblical Words for Feast

Unfortunately, the English Bible hides the full dimension of the word "feast" by translating three different Hebrew words into the single English word. Each Hebrew word, however, contributes to and expands the overall meaning of a Biblical feast. The three Biblical Hebrew words for feast and their meaning are:

- *Misteh* -- Generic term for feast
- *Hag* -- Specific feasts, the Pilgrimage Feasts
- *Moed* -- Appointment between God and Israel

The first word, *misteh*, is the most generic term for feast. It conveys the idea of a gathering to honor an important personage, usually with a meal. For example, in Genesis 19 Abraham honors three "men" (two angels and the pre-incarnate Jesus Christ) by hastily preparing a meal as the men rest before continuing their journey to Sodom. Notice that the meal was an impromptu affair since Abraham did not know that the men were coming. On this occasion the meal served as an element of secondary importance. The primary element lay in Abraham's honoring his guests. *Misteh* does include a spiritual element, however, since God gave Abraham a number of spiritual instructions on this occasion.

The book of Job records that Job observed a *misteh* with his sons on their birthdays. On each of these occasions he prepared a birthday meal (Job 1:4) and called the family together to honor that person. Verse 5 tells us that Job introduced a spiritual emphasis on these joyous occasions by offering sacrifices. From *misteh* we see, therefore, that a feast of this type is a spiritual gathering, either planned or impromptu, to honor a chosen person. Since both Job and Abraham lived long before the formal beginning of the nation of Israel, we know that *misteh* was in common usage and not exclusively used of the seven Feasts of the LORD.

The second word for feast, *hag*, both expands and narrows the meaning of *misteh*. Of the seven Feasts of Israel, *hag* refers to only three specific feasts: the Feasts of Unleavened Bread, Pentecost, and Tabernacles. With regards to these feasts, God commanded

> *Three times in a year shall all thy males appear before the LORD thy God in the place which he shall choose; in the feast of unleavened bread, and in the feast of weeks [Pentecost], and in the feast of tabernacles; and they shall not appear before the LORD empty.*
> Deuteronomy 16:16

As a result of this command, the Jewish people call these three feasts the Pilgrimage Feasts. On these occasions, God required the men of Israel to come to Jerusalem to honor Him by offering sacrifices (i.e. *"they shall not appear before the LORD empty"*). Once again, as in a *misteh*, these feasts involve a gathering together for spiritual purposes. *Hag* expands the idea by adding the element of a *specific* feast, commanded by God, in which the men of Israel honor God by their attendance.

When Moses first confronted Pharaoh (Exodus 5:1), he requested permission to take the Hebrews out into the wilderness to observe a *hag* (a pilgrimage feast).

> *And afterward Moses and Aaron went in, and told Pharaoh, Thus saith the LORD God of Israel, Let my people go, that they may hold a feast [hag] unto me in the wilderness.*

4

When Pharaoh refused, God used ten plagues to bring about the deliverance of the Hebrews whom He subsequently formed into the nation of Israel. God commanded the Hebrews to come to Him and hold a feast "*unto me*" in this use of *hag*. Note also, that Pharaoh did not ask Moses to define *hag;* he merely asked "*Who is the* LORD*, that I should obey his voice to let Israel go?*" (Exodus 5:2). Since many ancient writings mention feasts to various gods, Pharaoh clearly understood the concept of a *hag*. His refusal probably stems from the fact that he wanted the honor that the Hebrews owed to their LORD.

Hag narrows the meaning of *misteh* by referring only to feasts decreed by God in their "*season*" (Leviticus 23:4). *Hag* therefore eliminates the impromptu nature of a *misteh*. The word "*season*," Biblically speaking, literally means "appointed time." God appointed the Feasts as national events in much the same way as He appointed the events of Ecclesiastes 3. God not only demands that His people attend the Feasts, He also superintends the circumstances surrounding them.

> *I know that, whatsoever God doeth, it shall be for ever: nothing can be put to it, nor any thing taken from it: and God doeth it, that men should fear before Him.*
>
> Ecclesiastes 3:14

Just as with a dental appointment, Israel must observe the Feasts at the appointed date and time. On four of the seven feasts, Israel experienced major national "mountain-top" events. Only God could prearrange circumstances in such a way. God controls Israel just as He controls the rise and fall of other nations around the world. Daniel tells Nebuchadnezzar, the great king of Babylon, "*that the Most High ruleth in the kingdom of men and giveth it to whomsoever he will*" (Daniel 4:25). This passage points out the fact that God controls the circumstances that create world events and uses them for His own purpose. That purpose includes revealing His personality to us.

The third Hebrew word for feast, *moed*, demonstrates God's total control over circumstances. *Moed* comes from the word "betrothal." In ancient times, the bride and groom's parents prearranged the wedding of their children while the bride and groom had little say in the matter. Aside from being present at the appointed time, they had few duties. Their parents, on the other hand, chose the participants and set the time and place. In a *moed* God plans all the details and shapes history in order to bring about each appointment. Reflecting this theme, God called the Tabernacle the "*tent of meeting* or *appointment*" (Numbers 10:3 - literal meaning - *Online Bible Hebrew Lexicon*, 04150). At this appointed place and time, Moses would sound two silver trumpets to call the people of Israel to gather to meet with their God.

Moed fully defines a feast as a gathering of God's people to honor God and to see God manifested before them. **A Biblical Feast of the LORD is a unique appointment, set by God Himself; to meet with Israel at His designated times.** It also exists to teach mankind spiritual truths about its Creator. God chose seven such appointments to demonstrate how these truths apply to the nation of Israel as well as to individual people. As we study the past and future history of Israel, we discover seven definitive moments in Israel's history, one connected with each Feast. From the perspective of today we see that four such moments have already occurred, and three are yet to come.

Hebrew Word	Biblical Meaning
misteh	A spiritual gathering, either planned or impromptu, to honor a chosen person.
Hag	*Specific* feasts [called the Pilgrimage Feasts - Unleavened Bread, Weeks/Pentecost, and Tabernacles] commanded by God, in which the **men** of Israel honor God by their required attendance and offerings.
moed	A spiritual gathering or appointment of God's people, **Israel**, to honor God and to see God **manifested** before them.

Figure 2 – Feast Word Definitions

In planning the seven Feasts, God also appointed the time relationship among them. Like the Feasts themselves, these time relationships teach important truths. In order to understand these truths, however, we must first understand the calendars of the Bible so that these relationships will come into sharp focus. A close study shows that the Bible mentions **four different calendars**. The reader must understand their relationships to each other, or he may well miss a significant event.

Calendars of the Bible

Our modern calendar, called the Gregorian calendar (which Pope Gregory modified from the Julian calendar of Roman days), uses the sun as its reference point. On the other hand, all of the calendars mentioned in the Bible use the moon as their reference. Through Psalm 104:19 God makes it clear that He designed the moon for just such a purpose. *"He appointed the moon for seasons: the sun knoweth his going down."* Unfortunately, the solar and lunar systems work very differently making Biblical dating rather difficult for us accustomed as we are to a solar calendar. For this reason, any Bible study involving dates requires us to understand the lunar calendar.

<u>**Solar Calendar Systems**</u>
Present Day Calendar

<u>**Lunar Calendar Systems of the Bible**</u>
Mosaic or Biblical Calendar
Abib Calendar
Pre-Exilic or Phoenician Calendar
Post-Exilic or Babylonian Calendar

The **first lunar calendar** mentioned in the Bible is the Mosaic Calendar which is also known as the Hebrew or Biblical Calendar. In this calendar, God established twelve months, each of which He numbered starting with the opening month of the year, logically called the "First Month." Incidentally, the First Month comes in the spring unlike our January which comes in the winter. The "Second Month" follows the First Month with the calendar continuing on through the "Twelfth Month." Exodus 12:2 first mentions the Mosaic Calendar: *"This month shall be unto you the beginning of months; it shall be the first month of the year to you."*

God probably chose numerical month names in order to distinguish His calendar from those of the pagan nations around Israel. Most other ancient cultures named their months after their various deities, a practice foreign to the monotheistic Hebrews. Pagan nations also usually placed their New Year in the autumn for religious reasons connected with fertility rites. God, again desiring to make His calendar distinct, placed the first month of the year in the spring. Passover, the first feast, occurs in the middle of this initial month. On our solar calendar this time falls sometime in either March or April. *Figure 3* shows the relationship of the four Biblical calendars to the modern Gregorian calendar used today.

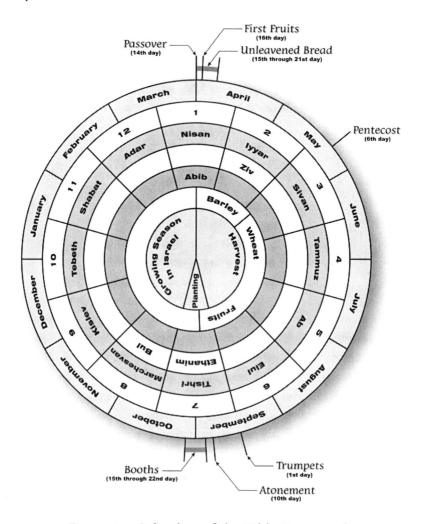

Figure 3 – Calendars of the Bible Compared

8

In Israel the harvest begins near the start of the year. Barley ripens first followed by wheat about seven weeks later. Minor crops such as fruits and grapes come last at the end of the wheat harvest. Planting begins after the final harvest. The crops then grow during what are for us winter months (in this book all of the references to the seasons are based upon the North American seasons; different parts of the world experience their seasons at other times of the year depending upon their hemisphere and general climate).

Frequently, the Bible refers to the early and the late rains. The early rains give the seeds their start during the critical germination phase of growth. The "latter rains" are those rains that, coming just before the harvest, give that final "burst" of growth to the harvest. When Israel fell out of fellowship with God, He withheld these critical rains to remind them of their spiritually weak condition. On the other hand, when the nation remained in close fellowship with its God, He blessed them according to the Mosaic Covenant:

> *And it shall come to pass, if ye shall hearken diligently unto my commandments which I command you this day, to love the LORD your God, and to serve him with all your heart and with all your soul, that I will give you the rain of your land in his due season, the first rain and the latter rain, that thou mayest gather in thy corn, and thy wine, and thine oil. . . . And then the LORD's wrath be kindled against you, and he shut up the heaven, that there be no rain, and that the land yield not her fruit.*
>
> Deuteronomy 11:13-17

The Feasts themselves occur during the first seven months of the year. Passover, the Feast of Unleavened Bread and the Feast of First Fruits fall in the First Month. Pentecost falls in the Third Month. The Feast of Trumpets, the Day of Atonement, and the Feast of Tabernacles appear in the Seventh Month, rounding off the yearly celebration of the Feasts. Because God often uses agricultural images in connection with the Feasts, we must understand the relationships of the seasons, the crops, and the rain patterns in order to understand the Feasts fully. Additionally, we must understand the relationships among the other calendars in order to detect all of the significant historical relationships in the Feasts, particularly, the Feast of Trumpets.

Scholars call **the second lunar calendar** used in the Bible the Abib Calendar. Like the Mosaic calendar, this calendar also begins in the spring. Scholars believe that the Abib Calendar comes down to us from a long-forgotten civilization. Beyond this speculation, we know very little about it. The Bible mentions the Abib calendar only four times (Exodus 13:4; 23:15; 34:18; Deuteronomy 16:1). On each occasion the passage mentions the calendar in connection with the Exodus on Passover.

The third calendar, known as the Pre-Exilic or Phoenician Calendar, names its months after a series of common Phoenician names. The Bible mentions only three months from this calendar: Ziv, Ethanim, and Bul. All references appear in 1 Kings 6 and 8 in connection with the building and dedication of Solomon's Temple. This mention is logical since Solomon used skilled Phoenician craftsmen to design and build his temple. Since the record keepers of the project were probably also Phoenician, their use of the Phoenician calendar seems quite natural. Furthermore, since Phoenicia dominated the commercial trading world during this time, its language acted as a sort of *lingua franca* for the ancient world.

The fourth calendar, the Post-Exilic or Babylonian Calendar appears frequently in the post-exilic books of the Bible. The Hebrews returning from their seventy-year exile brought many of the Babylonian ways back to Israel including the Babylonian Calendar. The books of Ezra, Nehemiah, Esther, and Zechariah all refer to this calendar and often cross-reference it to the Mosaic calendar (Esther 8:9 is a good example). *Figure 3* shows a combined calendar that incorporates all four of the ancient calendars, our modern Gregorian calendar, the agricultural cycle, and the positions of the Feasts.

Just as we use a calendar to tell us the date of our next dental appointment, so too, we can use the seven Feasts of the Lord to determine where we are on God's timetable. Israel will keep these appointments as God brings them about through His control of the times and circumstances. Since God has already fulfilled four of the seven appointments, we can feel assured that the other three will also come to pass. At the same time, we can also avoid the mistakes and fallacies that "date setters" fall into through misinterpretation of Biblical events. Furthermore, by studying the four fulfilled appointments, we can also learn much about our God, His personality, and His dealings with mankind.

CHAPTER 2:
OVERVIEW OF THE FEASTS

Speak unto the children of Israel, and say unto them, concerning the feasts of the LORD, which ye shall proclaim to be holy convocations, even these are my feasts.

Leviticus 23:2

A true understanding of the seven Feasts of the LORD requires a general understanding of the timing and method by which the nation of Israel observed (and still observes) the Feasts. This chapter provides a basic "grounding" by presenting a brief overview of each feast. Readers already familiar with the essentials of the Feasts may wish to proceed to Chapter 3. The following chapters cover the theological significance of these feasts. This chapter focuses on the "ritual" aspects of each feast.

Following the exodus of the Hebrews from Egypt, the LORD led the people into the wilderness east of Egypt. About fifty days later, He presented the Law, which functioned as the constitution for the new nation of Israel. As a part of the Law, God commanded the observance of seven yearly feasts which He grouped into three clusters. Two clusters contain three feasts each while the one contains but a single feast. As a part of the regulations governing the Feasts, God commanded all Jewish males to gather together on three specific feasts. Further, God indicated that they must gather at the "*place which He shall choose*" (Deuteronomy 16:16). Years later God designated Jerusalem as the "chosen place" of gathering. Because the men had to journey to this location, the feasts that brought about this gathering became known as the Pilgrimage Feasts. All seven of the Feasts occur during the first seven months of the Jewish year. God named each feast and ordained its date in Leviticus 23:4.

First Month Feasts
- **Passover**
- **Feast of Unleavened Bread**
- **Feast of First Fruit**

Third Month Feast
- **Pentecost [Feast of Weeks]**

Seventh Month Feasts
- **Feast of Trumpets**
- **Day of Atonement**
- **Feast of Tabernacles**

Although God ordained only seven feasts, modern Israel observes additional ones that have come about as a result of later traditions. Of these additional feasts, the Bible recognizes only two: Purim and Hanukkah. It never suggests, however, that God initiated them or commanded their observance. Jesus Christ apparently accepted their observance since the Gospels mention the fact that He participated in them on several occasions. We must always remember, however, that the added feasts originate from man rather than from God. Although the "extra" feasts, which usually commemorate events in Jewish history, may be historically interesting, they do not have the same God-ordained status as the original seven. For this reason, this book does not address these feasts in detail.

The First Feast: Passover

Ninety-nine percent of the modern Israeli population observes Passover each year. In AD 65, "not less than three millions" observed it (Kolatch 184-185). The observance of Passover involves Jewish people from all periods of history. Passover stands as one of the greatest historic events in the history of Israel, representing the birth of the nation out of the slavery of Egypt. The Hebrew Scriptures (the Old Testament) frequently allude to it. In many ways, Passover offers the key to understanding Judaism. In Leviticus 23:5, God gives cursory Passover instructions when He enumerates the Feasts: "*In the fourteenth day of the first month at even is the LORD's Passover.*" This passage mentions only the date and time of the feast. For more thorough information one must read Genesis 12 through Exodus 13 in order to understand the events surrounding the Passover. While the instructions of Leviticus 23 are brief, Passover's observance is not.

Since Passover is essentially a family event, Jewish people observe it in the home. The family gathers around the table to observe the *Haggadah*, or "showing forth." This term matches that used in 1 Corinthians 11:26: "*For as often as ye eat this bread, and drink this cup, ye do show* [forth] *the Lord's death till he come.*" Scripture and tradition lay out every step of the observance (Numbers 9:3). The Passover dinner lasts two to three hours during which time the host recites the history of the Egyptian slavery and God's great deliverance. Four cups of wine and unleavened bread symbolically picture the significance of Passover. The Friends of Israel Gospel Ministries publication *Passover Haggadah* offers an excellent overview of the Passover ritual.

Preparation for the Passover includes removing all leaven from the house prior to the event. This action symbolically frees the sacred event from the presence of sin and uncleanness. According to the Bible, only Hebrews and proselytes may participate in the event. In Exodus 12:11 God gave the following instructions: "*Thus shall ye eat it; with your loins girded, your shoes on your feet, your staff in your hand; and ye shall eat it in haste; it is the LORD's Passover.*" Today the celebration, a relaxed event, extends over seven or eight days.

Unfortunately, in modern times, Jewish people often combine Passover with the next two feasts, Unleavened Bread and First Fruits, thereby clouding the individual significance of each feast. The fear of bondage and persecution remains in the mind of the observer, however. Modern Passover reminds each generation of the "importance of continuing the battle for freedom" (Kolatch 182). In Chapter 3, we will look at the Biblical purpose for the Passover.

The Second Feast: Unleavened Bread

As already noted, modern Jews combine this feast with the Passover. The Scriptures, however, clearly maintain Unleavened Bread's status as a distinct and separate feast.

And on the fifteenth day of the same month is the feast of unleavened bread unto the LORD: seven days ye must eat unleavened bread. In the first day ye shall have a holy convocation: ye shall do no servile work therein. But ye shall offer an offering made by fire unto the LORD seven days: in the seventh day is a holy convocation: ye shall do no servile work therein.

Leviticus 23:6-8

Unlike Passover which occupies but a single day, Unleavened Bread spans a seven-day period. The feast begins and ends with a sabbath (days of worship that exclude any servile [unnecessary] work). The very name of the feast emphasizes the exclusive nature of the bread involved in its observance. The use of unleavened bread derives from the hasty departure from Egypt which prevented the preparation of normal (leavened) bread. By eating unleavened bread over the seven days of the feast, the Jewish people remind themselves of the hasty departure from Egypt as well as the journey that followed.

Since Passover and Unleavened bread fall in close proximity to one another (one day apart to be exact), a clear connection emerges. Andrew Bonar says, "Passover was the cause, the feast of unleavened bread the effects, of their deliverance from the grasp of Egypt" (389). For this reason, we forever associate these two feasts with the birth of Israel and the exodus from Egypt.

Unlike Passover, which they observe in their homes, Jewish people observe the Feast of Unleavened Bread by gathering together as a nation on the first and second Sabbaths of the feast. The feast represents a community of people celebrating their common escape and separation from the land of Egypt with its spiritual pollution and corruption (Bonar 390). Note, however, that these Sabbaths are *not* the regular weekly Sabbaths (Saturdays). The "Sabbaths" of Unleavened Bread fall according to *date* rather than day of the week and may therefore fall upon days other than Saturday.

The first Sabbath serves as a time for special offerings, worship, meditation, rest, and preparation for the five "ordinary" days of the feast. The celebrants spend the five days between the two Sabbaths joyfully performing their daily tasks, remembering that they must cherish the freedom to work as they wish and not according to the whims of their

Egyptian taskmasters. Although they work as usual on the five middle days, the people begin each day with a sacrifice to the LORD (Leviticus 23:8). The last Sabbath completes the feast with meditation, worship, rest, and special offerings to the LORD. Additionally, Scripture stipulates that *"Every man shall give as he is able, according to the blessing of the LORD thy God which he hath given thee"* (Deuteronomy 16:17).

God gave one final instruction which makes this feast well worth noting. He required every Jewish male to attend this feast *"in the place which He shall choose . . . and they shall not appear before the LORD empty"* (Deuteronomy 16:16). This command marks the Feast of Unleavened Bread as one of the three "Pilgrimage Feasts" which we have already mentioned. Scripture commands all Jewish males, regardless of where they are in the world, to make a pilgrimage up to Jerusalem for this feast. Today, few men outside of Israel follow this command.

The Third Feast: First Fruits

The barley harvest of Israel begins on the 16th day of the First Month, the Feast of First Fruits. The LORD instructs,

> *Speak unto the children of Israel, and say unto them, When ye be come into the land which I give unto you, and shall reap the harvest thereof, then ye shall bring a sheaf of the first fruits of your harvest unto the priest: And he shall wave the sheaf before the LORD, to be accepted for you: on the morrow after the Sabbath the priest shall wave it.*
>
> Leviticus 23:10-12

The Scriptures most closely connect the Feast of First Fruits and the Feast of Pentecost to agricultural Israel. On this spring day, Israeli farmers begin to gather the barley harvest of the land. Before gathering barley for themselves, however, the farmers gather their first fruits for the LORD (Exodus 23:19). Much as we give of a tithe of our earnings to the Lord, so too, the Jewish farmer gives a tithe of his crops. Nationally, officials of the Sanhedrin gather a sheaf (approximately 3 ½ pecks) of barley at the start of the Feast of First Fruits. The priests at the Temple then "wave" the sheaf and then carefully thresh and grind the grain into one omer of flour. Interestingly, when the priest waves the sheaf, the pattern takes the form of a Roman cross. They then make the flour into a loaf of unleavened bread and place it in the Temple before the LORD. The people believe that this sheaf represents the best of the coming harvest, a symbol of plenty to come.

Leviticus 23:14 declares the Feast of First Fruits a perpetual feast of Israel. For this reason, it will continue throughout history. Observance, however, depends upon Israel's presence in the land and its covenant relationship with God.

The Fourth Feast: Pentecost (Feast of Weeks or Harvest)

Scripture does not specify a specific day of the month for the Feast of Pentecost, known also as the Feast of Weeks (Deuteronomy 16:10) and the Feast of Harvest (Exodus 23:16). Instead, Israel observes the Feast of Pentecost fifty days after the Feast of First Fruits. For this reason, the name "Pentecost" comes from the Greek work for fifty, "penthkosth" (Freeman 909).

> *And you shall count unto you from the morrow after the Sabbath, from the day that ye brought the sheaf of the wave offering; seven Sabbaths shall be complete: even unto the morrow after the seventh Sabbath shall ye number fifty days; and ye shall offer a new meat offering unto the LORD. Ye shall bring out of your habitations two wave loaves of two tenth deals: they shall be of fine flour; they shall be baked with leaven; they are the first fruits unto the LORD.*
> Leviticus 23:15-17

During the forty-nine days (and seven Sabbaths) between First Fruits and Pentecost, the farmers gather their crops of barley and process them. At Pentecost, Israel begins harvesting its second principal crop, wheat. Once again, as a part of their observance of the feast, they bring the "first fruit" offering to the LORD. Once again, officials gather a sheaf and wave it before the LORD.

In the same way as it does on the Feast of First Fruits, Scripture prohibits servile work on this day of thanksgiving and rejoicing (Numbers 28:26). Once again, this feast enables individuals to bring a freewill offering to the LORD as an expression of their gratitude in acknowledgment of His ownership of all (Deuteronomy 16:10).

your God. For whatsoever soul it be that shall not be afflicted in that same day, he shall be cut off from among his people. And whatsoever soul it be that doeth any work in that same day, the same soul will I destroy from among his people. Ye shall do no manner of work: it shall be a statute for ever throughout your generations in all your dwellings. It shall be unto you a Sabbath of rest [Sabbath Sabbath - literally], *and ye shall afflict your souls: in the ninth day of the month at even, form even unto even, shall ye celebrate your Sabbath.*

Leviticus 23:27-32

The solemnity of the day comes from the strict restrictions regarding work and the need to afflict the soul. God, indicating the seriousness of the occasion, decrees that anyone who works during the day must die (Leviticus 23:30). The term "Sabbath of rest," a very rare term, appears in connection with this feast. This phrase, used only six times in the Bible, speaks of ultimate rest or the ceasing from daily activities of toil and struggle.

On this day, Israel offers a *"kid of the goats for a sin offering; beside the offering of atonement"* (Numbers 29:11). Leviticus 16 contains most of the instructions regarding the spiritual offerings. These include two goats, of which one serves as the sin offering and sheds its blood to cleanse the holy things and the people (Leviticus 16:5, 9). The High Priest takes the blood of the first goat and carries it into the Holy of Holies to make atonement for the people and for the Tabernacle or Temple (Leviticus 16:15, 16). The second goat, the scapegoat, makes atonement for the High Priest and for his house (Leviticus 16:10). Following the cleansing of the Temple and the people, the priest leads the scapegoat into the wilderness and frees it (Leviticus 16:20-22). The Bible says that the atonement serves *"to cleanse you, that ye may be clean from all your sins before the LORD"* (Leviticus 16:30). With the close of this solemn day, Israel prepares for the joyous celebration of the next feast.

The Seventh Feast: Tabernacles (Feast of Booths)

Speaking for many, a rabbi once said, "He who has not seen Jerusalem during the Feast of Tabernacles does not know what rejoicing means" (Buksbazen 46). Last of the three Pilgrimage Feasts, the Feast of

Tabernacles, and beginning on the fifteenth day of the Seventh Month, concludes the yearly cycle of feasts.

> *Also in the fifteenth day of the seventh month, when ye have gathered in the fruit of the land, ye shall keep a feast unto the LORD seven days: on the first day shall be a Sabbath, and on the eighth day shall be a sabbath. And ye shall take you on the first day the boughs of goodly trees, branches of palm trees, and the boughs of thick trees, and willows of the brook; and ye shall rejoice before the LORD your God seven days. And ye shall keep it a feast unto the LORD seven days in the year. It shall be a statute for ever in your generations: ye shall celebrate it in the seventh month. Ye shall dwell in booths seven days; all that are Israelites born shall dwell in booths: that your generations may know that I made the children of Israel to dwell in booths; when I brought them out of the land of Egypt: I am the LORD your God.*
>
> Leviticus 23:39-43

Israel celebrates this feast for seven days, starting and ending with a Sabbath as was done for the Feast of Unleavened Bread. A true Israelite constructs a booth (*sukka*) of palms where he takes his meals. During the Temple Period the people waved palm branches and recited Psalms as a part of the feast's celebration. Modern Jews see this feast as a celebration of their forty-year journey from the Wilderness to the Promised Land. For this reason, they construct the *sukka* as a temporary dwelling thereby teaching the lesson that man lives an insecure and temporary life in this world. The feast also includes a service at the end of which the people form a procession and march while singing Psalm 118. This tradition began in the Temple days with the singing of songs like the following:

We beseech Thee, O Lord, save now!
We beseech Thee, O Lord, make us now to prosper!

(Kolatch 254)

Unlike the Day of Atonement which precedes it, the Feast of Tabernacles causes much joy and singing. The Scriptures play a large part in the observance. In ancient times on the second day of the feast, a priest carried water from the Pool of Siloam in Jerusalem and poured it out upon the altar. The people followed the priest singing, dancing, and carrying torches in procession. Some see this ceremony as a symbolic petition for the early rains for the next harvest. The Talmud (Mishna Sukkot 5:1) says "He who has not witnessed the Celebration of the Libation of Water has never seen merriment in his life."

Some confusion exists over the number of days in this feast. Leviticus 23:41 mentions the feast as a seven-day feast, but Leviticus 23:39 mentions an eighth day. Scholars hold two views on this subject. Some contend that the feast lasts for eight days, while others speculate that an unnamed feast follows the seven-day Feast of Tabernacles. As Chapter 10 will explain, the phrase "Sabbath of rest" reveals the answer to this dilemma and ties the Feast of Tabernacles to the grand finale of time, the Great Jubilee.

Other Feasts Historic and Modern (non-Biblical)

Simchat Torah

A joyful holiday observed in both home and synagogue, Simchat Torah commemorates the Torah, the teaching and doctrine given in the five books of Moses. It literally means "rejoicing over the law." Jewish people celebrate it on the 23rd day of Tishri

Hanukkah

This holiday came about as a result of the great Maccabean military victory in 168 BC over the Seleucid ruler Antiochus Epiphanes. On the 25th day of Kislev, Antiochus profaned the Temple by sacrificing a pig upon the altar. Exactly three years later under Judas Maccabeus, the Jewish army reclaimed the Temple, cleansed it, and re-dedicated it to the true God. A happy time of family gatherings, meals, and activities, Hanukkah incorporates a nine-branch menorah to commemorate the eight days of the Temple re-dedication during which a one-day supply of dedication oil miraculously burned for a full eight days (a tradition only, unfortunately). Hanukkah literally means "dedication." Beginning on the 25th day of Kislev, modern Jewish people celebrate the feast for eight days, marking each day by lighting another branch of the menorah.

Purim

This holiday commemorates the time when God delivered the Jewish people from near destruction through Queen Esther's intercession. During King Ahasuerus' rule during the early post-exilic time, Haman, a royal official who hated the Jewish people, created a decree to bring about their destruction. God, working through Mordecai and Queen Esther, exposed Haman's evil plan to the king. While he could not reverse his decree, the king did permit the Jewish people to defend themselves against attack. Their enemies saw the tide turn and spared the Jewish people. On this happiest holiday of the year, people exchange food baskets and give monetary gifts to the poor. Children dress as queens, kings, and men using costumes and false beards. The people read the book of Esther in their synagogues and boo when they hear Haman's name. Following the service, they enjoy a festive meal in their homes. Purim is celebrated on the 14th day of Adar.

Yom Ha-Sho'ah

This recently added commemorative occasion marks the date of the Warsaw Ghetto uprising in 1943 and the Holocaust as a whole. Observers give wreaths as well as thoughts and words in tribute to the Holocaust victims. A siren blasts for two minutes calling all to stop and stand still in remembrance. In Israel the Jewish people observe this event on the 27th day of Nisan (in other countries Jews often observe it on different dates).

Yom ha-Atzma'ut

Observed on May 14, this event celebrates the beginning of the modern state of Israel which declared its independence on this date in 1948.

The Fifteenth of Av

Today few celebrate the Fifteenth of Av, a holiday started during the Second Temple Period. Those who celebrate the occasion, which commemorates a number of historical events in Israel's history, do so by reading the Bible and various rabbinical teachings.

The Fifteenth of Shevat

This day is Israel's Arbor Day, a day reflecting the greening of the land of Israel, once desolate as a result of the Roman invasion and destruction in AD 70.

For additional material on these holidays, particularly their ceremonies and traditions see *The Feasts of Israel* by Bruce Scott, published by The Friends of Israel Gospel Ministries.

CHAPTER 3:
THE PASSOVER

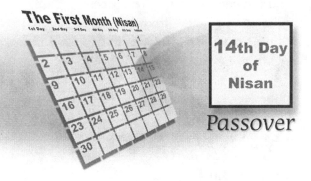

. . . when I see the blood, I will pass over you.

Exodus 12:13b

Without properly understanding the timing and history of the Feast of Passover, one cannot see its significance to the covenant history of Israel or its application to the Church. Victor Buksbazen states, "The deliverance of Israel from Egypt, is the central point in Jewish history and worship, even as Calvary is the central point in the Christian faith" (Buksbazen 2). While the Passover itself took place in Egypt, its true birth occurred long before in Mesopotamia with the man Abram of Ur. Since God's covenant promise to Abram underlines both the Passover and the remaining six feasts, we must thoroughly understand the nature of this covenant before we can study the Feasts. God chose Abram, a man living in a pagan, idol-filled world, simply because He loved him.

And because he loved thy fathers, therefore he chose their seed after them, and brought thee out in his sight with his mighty power out of Egypt.

Deuteronomy 4:37

Only the LORD had a delight in thy fathers to love them, and he chose their seed after them, even you above all people, as it is this day.

Deuteronomy 10:15

God's unconditional covenant centered upon His love for Abram which, in turn, resulted from His sovereign choice and not from any merit on Abram's part. In Genesis 12:3 God makes seven promises to Abram affirming that He will

Make him a great nation
Bless him
Make his name great
Make him a blessing
Bless those that bless him
Curse those that curse him
Bless all the families of the earth through him

The seven Feasts of the LORD symbolically picture the fulfillment of these promises. Throughout its history, God will meet with Israel on seven occasions (appointments), each memorialized by a feast. These historical appointments demonstrate His "active presence [to be] manifested [in] His character, power, and ability to fulfill the repeated word of promise. It was preeminently a word of personal relationship" (Kaiser 95). This relationship, beginning with Abram, spans human history, although its ultimate fulfillment is not yet complete. The writer of Hebrews, speaking at the start of the Church Age, states: "*These all died in faith, not having received the promises, but having seen them afar off, and were persuaded of them, and embraced them, and confessed that they were strangers and pilgrims on the earth*" (Hebrews 11:13). Those dead include Abraham, Isaac, and Jacob, men to whom God gave the promise. The currently unfulfilled promises clearly indicate the prophetic nature of several of the feasts.

After detailing the promises of the Covenant, God explains its national aspects:

> *. . . I am the Almighty God; walk before me, and be thou perfect. And I will make my covenant between me and thee, and will multiply thee exceedingly. . . . As for me, behold, my covenant is with thee, and thou shalt be a father of many nations. Neither shall thy name any more be called Abram, but thy name shall be Abraham; for a father of many nations have I made thee. . . and kings shall come out of thee. And I will establish my covenant between me and thee and thy seed after thee in their generations for an everlasting covenant, to be a God unto thee, and to thy seed after thee. And I will give unto thee, the land wherein thou art a stranger, all the land of Canaan, for an everlasting possession; and I will be their God.*
>
> Genesis 17:1-8

When God gave this promise, Abram had no son nor had he, due to his advanced age, the prospect of having one. He lived in Ur, a place far from the land of Canaan. When God referred to kings coming forth from Abram, He clearly touched upon one of the requirements of a nation. Kaiser points out,

> Just now it was a relationship with a man which served as a basis for blessing the people of the earth. Interesting enough, the actual realization of a promise such as nationhood would have to wait for several centuries until Israel was delivered from Egypt (Kaiser, 88).

God began to fulfill the promise by giving Abram a son, Isaac, through his wife Sarai. As a further sign of the promise, God changed Abram's name to Abraham. Years later, God perpetuates the promise through Isaac's son Jacob, whom he renames Israel.

And God said unto him, Thy name is Jacob: thy name shall not be called any more Jacob, but Israel shall be thy name: and he called his name Israel....I am God Almighty: be fruitful and multiply; a nation and a company of nations shall be of thee, and kings shall come out of thy loins; and the land which I gave Abraham, and Isaac, to thee I will give it, and to thy seed after thee will I give the land.

Genesis 35:10-12

God sovereignly directs Jacob's covenant family (now consisting of twelve sons) through his son Joseph to move to the land of Egypt. The "sojourn" in Egypt fulfilled a prophecy that God had given to Abraham indicating that his "*seed*" would someday be a "*stranger*" and "*serve*" in a foreign land for four-hundred years: "*And he said unto Abram, Know of a surety that thy seed shall be a stranger in a land that is not theirs, and shall serve them; and they shall afflict them four hundred years*" (Genesis 15:13).

God brought this prophecy to pass by providentially making Joseph, through a remarkable train of events, the "prime minister" of Egypt. Through the agency of a famine, God then drew the remainder of the family from Canaan to Egypt. Here the family lived and prospered. During its four-hundred year sojourn in Egypt, this "family" grew to between two and three million people. Genesis 50:26 through Exodus 1:1 records this period of history. After living 110 years, Joseph died in Egypt. As he approached death, Joseph, speaking by faith, mentioned God's promise:

...I die: and God will surely visit you, and bring you out of this land unto the land which he sware to Abraham, to Isaac, and to Jacob. . . . God will surely visit you, and ye shall carry my bones up from hence"

Genesis 50:24-25

God used the years in Egypt to transform this group of people from a large family into the infant nation of Israel. Before this transformation could happen, however, two conditions had to be met. First, Israel needed significant numerical growth. "Egypt afforded excellent living conditions for necessary rapid growth in numbers" (Wood 81). Second, a group, no matter how large, must be united. "To be called a 'people' . . . meant that they were an ethnic social group with enough numerical strength and enough unity to be regarded as a corporate whole" (Kaiser 103). For God to create this "corporate whole," He would have to separate them, mentally, emotionally, and physically, from the land in which they had lived for the past four-hundred years.

To make this separation easier, God placed them in the pagan, foreign Egyptian culture. The Hebrew occupation of shepherding, a profession abhorrent to the Egyptians, prevented further assimilation and limited intermarriage between the Egyptians and the Hebrews (Wood 103). God furthered the separation process by removing the Egyptian ruling party that had been favorable to the Hebrews and replacing it with a new group, the Hyksos. The Hyksos invasion of Egypt brought total subjection to the Egyptians and Hebrews alike (Rhea 7).

The Hyksos rule, which lasted for 150 years (1730-1570 BC), succeeded largely through its use of the chariot, the "tank" of the ancient world (De Vries 823). Eventually, the native Egyptians managed to overthrow and expel their Hyksos conquerors. They made good use of what they had learned about Hyksos military technology and used it to conquer and thereby acquire great national wealth. Ultimately, their acquired wealth financed not only Egypt but Israel as well.

"Now there arose up a new king over Egypt, which knew not Joseph" (Exodus 1:8). With this simple statement, the life of every Hebrew in Egypt changed drastically from one of honor to one of toil, subjection, and bondage (Wood 114). John Davis sums it up succinctly by saying, "For him [the Israelite] Egypt meant slavery and humiliation, and at the same time great victory and the birth of his nation" (15). Many of the Hebrews' experiences parallel man's spiritual journey through life. God used physical slavery to portray visually the invisible spiritual slavery from which every man needs deliverance. Until he feels the full weight of his bondage, man cannot appreciate his need for salvation.

The Egyptians, having acquired the oppressive ways of the Hyksos, turned on their Hebrew "guests" and enslaved them. Learning from their own overthrow by the Hyksos, the Egyptians grew fearful of the internal threat posed by their Hebrew slaves and issued the following edict: *"Therefore they did set over them taskmasters to afflict them with their burdens....And the Egyptians made the children of Israel to serve with rigor* [hardship]" (Exodus 1:11, 13). This single, economically motivated act negated the debt that the Hebrews owed to the Egyptians for the kindness they had received during Joseph's time. God often uses pagan world powers to advance His plans and purposes. Daniel remarks that *"and he changeth the times and the seasons: he removeth kings, and setteth up kings:..."* (Daniel 2:21).

The First Appointment with God: Passover

The Feast of Passover memorializes God's deliverance of Israel from slavery. In addition to its obvious physical significance, Passover also teaches us about the workings of spiritual deliverance. As God kept His first "appointment" with His people, God brought about the birth of a nation, the nation of Israel. God used Pharaoh and Moses to bring about this "birth."

The path of deliverance began when the Egyptian Sekenenre began a war of liberation against the Hyksos invaders. Ahmose I, the first king of the Eighteenth Dynasty, completed the process of liberation. During the Eighteenth Dynasty, Egypt reached the pinnacle of success and prosperity. Thutmose I succeeded Ahmose and substantially reduced the threat imposed by the neighboring Canaanite nations. Upon his death, Queen Hatshepsut seized power. Some speculate that she may have been the Pharaoh's daughter who found and adopted Moses (Wood 117-118). Thutmose III, "the greatest Pharaoh ever to occupy the throne of Egypt," eventually gained the throne from Hatshepsut (Hayes qtd. in Wood 118). During his reign, he intensified the oppression of the Hebrews. Moses probably fled Egypt at this time. If Hatshepsut **did** adopt Moses, such a relationship would explain Thutmose's general animosity toward Moses. Moses' murder of the Egyptian (Exodus 2:15) may have provided Thutmose with an excuse to revenge himself upon Moses (Davis 43). Thutmose's son, Amenhotep II, ascended the throne upon his father's death (Exodus 2:23) becoming the Pharaoh connected with the events of the Passover (Rhea 574).

God used Moses to found the new theocratic state and serve as the instrument of deliverance for the Hebrews (Rodgers 35). In His demonstration of deliverance, God would also judge the greatness of pagan Egypt and show that He reigns in justice over the enemies of His people. Characteristically, we find no mention of either Moses or the Exodus in Egyptian historical records. Charles Aling explains why:

> The peoples of the ancient Near East kept historical records to impress their gods and also potential enemies, and therefore rarely, if ever, mentioned defeats or catastrophes. Records of disasters would not enhance the reputation of the Egyptians in the eyes of their gods, nor make the enemies more afraid of their military might (qtd. in Davis 17).

God prefigured the coming national deliverance by providentially delivering Moses, the "deliverer" (Acts 7:35), from death in his infancy. *"By faith Moses, when he was born, was hid three months of his parents, because they saw he was a proper* [beautiful] *child; and they were not afraid of the king's commandment"* (Hebrews 11:23). Pharaoh's daughter (perhaps Hatshepsut) found the baby and gave him royal protection and upbringing. *"And Moses was learned in all the wisdom of the Egyptians, and was mighty in words and deeds"* (Acts 7:22). At the age of forty, Moses prematurely tried to become the "deliverer" apart from God's leading. His reckless action, the murder of an Egyptian, forced him to make a quick departure from Egypt. *"For he supposed his brethren would have understood how that God by his hand would deliver them; but they understood not"* (Acts 7:25). As early as Thutmose III's reign, the Hebrews called out for help and deliverance, something Moses tried unsuccessfully to deliver. The oppression continued for forty more years before time brought the Hebrews to their appointment with God.

God began this appointment by meeting with Moses in the wilderness at the burning bush (Exodus 3). God linked physical deliverance with spiritual deliverance:

> *I have surely seen the affliction of my people which are in Egypt, and have heard their cry by reason of their taskmasters; for I know their sorrows; and I am come down to deliver them out of the hand of the Egyptians, and to bring them up out of that land unto a good land.*
>
> Exodus 3:7, 8

The evidence of divine appointment lies in the words "*I have surely visited you*" (Exodus 3:16). God intended for His "*people the children of Israel*" (Exodus 3:10) to come out to the wilderness in order to "*sacrifice to the LORD*" (Exodus 3:18). God gave Moses and the people a token of assurance; upon their deliverance, they would return to "*serve God upon this mountain*" (Exodus 3:12), the same mountain (Mount Horeb, also known as Mount Sinai) where God had first instructed Moses concerning the coming deliverance.

Through this passage God established the first appointment (Passover) in which the people were to gather to honor Him by sacrifice at the appointed time. Such a sequence of events fits the definition of a *moed* or feast as defined in Chapter 1. Following the first historical appointment (Passover), God later ordained the remaining six feasts upon the very same Mount Sinai.

Two noteworthy observations arise concerning the Passover. First, the people did not seek an escape from Egypt; they merely wanted release from slavery. Second, they did not flee Egypt as refugees. God used the Egyptians to drive the Hebrews out of Egypt. At the same time, He also used the Egyptians to enrich the Israelites. His action demonstrates the fact that deliverance from slavery requires complete separation from the old life. In Exodus 6:1 God says, "*Then the Lord said unto Moses, Now shalt thou see what I will do to Pharaoh: for with a strong* [under compulsion] *hand shall he let them go, and with a strong hand shall he drive them out of his land*" God had to use Pharaoh to "*drive them out*" because the Hebrews were reluctant to leave. Over the next forty years, the Hebrews repeatedly tried to return to Egypt with its culture and its religion. The reluctance of the Hebrews to leave the world they knew demonstrates the difficulty of separating oneself spiritually from the world. From the standpoint of world history, this event stands out as unique. After all, what nation would willingly drive its slaves out of the country?

The Scriptural phrases "*land*" and "*my people*" demonstrate "the exciting story of Israel's deliverance from slavery and the beginning of her national identity" (Davis 15). This national identity and unity developed as a result of God's ten plagues or "*great judgments*" upon Egypt (Exodus 7:4). As the plagues increased in severity, they fostered increasing Egyptian resentment and thus greater oppression toward the

Hebrews. Notice that in these passages God calls the sons of Israel, "*My people*" for the very first time.

As he liberated the Hebrews, God simultaneously judged the enemies of the embryonic nation. "Since a kingdom of God was about to be established in history, it was essential that sinful men should be given historic evidence that Jehovah is the true God and sovereign over the nations" (McClain 55). The tenth judgment (the final plague) not only delivered the nation of Israel but, at the same time, also stood as a memorial to God's justice. "*The LORD had also executed judgment on their gods*" (Numbers 33:4). This historical appointment symbolizes a righteous man's deep need for God to remove him from the world and Satan's control. "The Hebrews were delivered not merely from outside foreign bondage, they were likewise rescued from inward spiritual degradation and sin" (Vos 111). The purposes of the Exodus, both positive and negative, demonstrate God's love for His people and His justice regarding sin. The Feast of Passover memorializes this great event.

The Day of Preparation and the Instructions for Passover

Exodus 12:3 specifies that the preparation for the Passover should begin "*on the tenth of this month.*" On the tenth day, the Day of Preparation, the people select the Passover lambs, carefully examining them for defects. Historically, Israel, under Joshua's leadership, entered the Promised Land on the tenth day of the First Month. Additionally, many (French 46, McClain 26) conclude that the Triumphal Entry happened on the same day of the month, Nisan 10, the Day of Preparation (Matthew 21:10-19, Luke 19:45-48, Mark 11:12-18). John 12 substantiates this conclusion when it mentions that Jesus shared a meal with Lazarus on the day before Palm Sunday (which came six days before the Passover), the ninth day of the First Month.

> *On the next day* [the tenth] *the great multitude who had come to the feast, when they heard that Jesus was coming to Jerusalem, took branches of the palm trees and went out*
>
> John 12:12-13

On the Day of Preparation when the people selected their lambs, Jesus spoke of judgment: "*Now judgment has come upon this world; now the ruler of this world shall be cast out. And I, if I be lifted up from the earth will draw all men to Myself*" (John 12:31). In verse 40 Jesus quoted Isaiah 6:10 concerning the blindness of Israel and the judgment to come. The context of this passage covers the spiritual deliverance offered by God as well as His judgment toward those who refuse that deliverance.

Passover instructions state that on the tenth day of the First Month the people select their sacrificial lambs and test them for blemishes. As instructed by Exodus 12:3, they choose one lamb for each household. So too on Palm Sunday, the people selected Jesus Christ as the Lamb that they would sacrifice on the coming Passover. 1 Corinthians 5:7 says, "*Purge out therefore the old leaven, that ye may be a new lump, as ye are unleavened. For even Christ our passover is sacrificed for us.*"

The family keeps the chosen lamb for four days (Exodus 12:6) and kills it just before Passover begins at sunset. God instructed Moses to take the sacrificed lamb's blood and sprinkle it upon the lintel and the door posts (12:7, 22). "As we stand back and see that blood in the shape of a cross: top, right and left sides, and bottom, we are reminded of those who have put their trust in the crucified, buried and risen Savior" (Rodgers 37).

Events of Passover – Day of the Week						
1st	2nd	3rd	4th	5th	6th	7th
Nisan 9	Nisan 10	Nisan 11	Nisan 12	Nisan 13	Nisan 14	Nisan 15
	Selection of the Lamb			Sacrifice of the Lamb	Passover	

Figure 4 – Events of Passover

On the original Passover the blood protected the firstborn son of the household from the Destroyer. The LORD instructed Moses, "*when I see the blood I will pass over you*" (Exodus 12:13). On that night God either destroyed or delivered the firstborn of the house. He **individually** met with each family, house by house, at this appointment and "*passed over*" those who had placed their trust in Him by faith in the blood. This event brought them into a new relationship with God and with the nation as a whole. Deliverance, therefore, depended upon obedience: "*ye shall say, It is the sacrifice of the LORD's passover, who passed over the houses of the children of Israel in Egypt, when He smote the Egyptians, and delivered our houses*" (Exodus 12:27).

This picture shows that God withholds death (in this case physical death) whenever He sees the shed, innocent blood of the substitute lamb. God declares the Passover a permanent memorial: "*And this day shall be unto you for a memorial; and ye shall keep it a feast to the LORD throughout your generations; ye shall keep it a feast by an ordinance for ever*" (Exodus 12:14). The Bible defines a memorial as an event "to remember, recall, call to mind usually as affecting present feelings, thought or action" (Brown et al. 269). "For the Hebrew the recollection of the past means that what is recalled becomes a present reality, which in turn controls the will" (Davies 3:344). The Passover memorial, therefore, reminds one of what God has done, while the memory motivates one to a response affecting his future. R. K. Harrison points out that "the passover . . . served as a valuable annual period of instruction, reminding the Israelites of the theological issues involved in the exodus from Egypt, and also the implications of covenant relationship" (217). The deliverance of the Hebrews during the Passover night gave birth to the nation of Israel. The nation enjoyed a unique personal relationship with God because of the "death/Passover" experience. The first element of the Covenant had been fulfilled; a great nation had been born.

The Biblical definition of "memorial" plays a vital role as we try to understand how the Scriptures use the word in relation to the Feasts. The meaning will become especially important when we examine the Feast of Trumpets (Chapter 7). In summary, a memorial contains the following elements:

- **One looks back at a past event**
- **One's thoughts are stimulated by that memory**
- **A response results from those thoughts and memories**

The Hebrew memorial not only looks back to the past but also motivates present and future actions. God uses Biblical memorials to bring about a desired spiritual response in the present. Andrew Bonar sees this aspect of a memorial demonstrated in the Passover: "Our heavenly Father has condescended to teach his children by most expressive pictures; and, even in this, much of his love appears" (7).

The significance of the Passover memorial demands that it be a permanent ordinance for the Hebrews. In contrast, Christ commands the Church to observe the Lord's Supper only "*till He come*" (1 Corinthians 11:26). The Lord instituted the Lord's Supper (Luke 22) on the Jewish Passover, identifying Himself as the true Passover Lamb, selected on Palm Sunday, and killed at Passover. Through His shed innocent blood, He provided the means for God the Father to "pass over" true Christians in terms of spiritual death (spiritual separation from God).

Passover became the focal point of Jewish history because it crystallized the Jewish national identity and marked the birth of the Jews as a free people. Due to the lessons gained from the experiences of Egyptian slavery and redemption, it also provided a powerful basis for many important concepts of the Jewish faith and ethic (Donin 218). Passover began the progressive fulfillment of the Abrahamic Covenant and, by so doing, also started the great prophetic clock of Israel. Just as an infant experiences a new freedom at its birth, so too did the former slaves experience a new freedom at that first Passover. Since Passover was the first appointment between God and Israel, God chose an appropriate symbol worthy of representing the event. The Passover month would mark the first month of the calendar year. "*This month shall be the beginning of months for you; it is to be the first month of the year to you*" (Exodus 12:2).

The Doctrinal Teaching

Passover marks the beginning of the nation of Israel to both the ancient and modern Jew. The Passover "commemorated the deliverance of the enslaved Israelites from Egypt by a mighty act of divine redemption and marked the establishing of the offspring of Jacob as a nation" (Harrison 216). This national beginning fulfilled the first aspect of the Abrahamic Covenant.

And what one nation in the earth is like thy people, even like Israel, whom God went to redeem for a people to himself, and to make him a name, and to do for you great things and terrible, for thy land, before thy people, which thou redeemest to thee from Egypt, from the nations and their gods?

2 Samuel 7:23

God made this beginning even more glorious because the Exodus took place during the height of Egyptian power, prestige, and glory. The timing of the event revealed the value of God's love for His people and His power to fulfill His covenant promises (Kaiser 104). To the Gentile nations, including Egypt, the event proclaimed three facts:

- **The absolute sovereignty of God over other alleged gods**
- **The selection of Israel as God's favored nation above all other nations**
- **The divine authority of Moses as the accredited mediator of God's word and will**

(McClain 54)

Deliverance and redemption touched the Israelites individually but also unified a nation of two million (Rodgers 38). The nation now needed formal organization and its own land. This organization came at Mt. Sinai where the constitution (the Law) defined the formal religious observances, the government, and Israel's relationship with its personal, covenant-keeping God. Regardless of the complexity of these covenantal laws, the simple plan of deliverance embodied in the Passover would remain etched forever in the minds of the Hebrews.

The firstborn of each family would certainly always remember the significance of Passover. God "thus prepared a type of the truth that a delivered, redeemed man must shake off his former connexion [sic] with pollution. His deliverance from corruption (leaven) is to date its commencement from the very hour he rises to forsake his house of bondage" (Bonar 390). The picture takes on a greater significance in the light of Calvary. At the Cross Jesus Christ offered deliverance and redemption to any man willing to trust Him and accept His payment for sins. In redemption God pays the ransom owed as a consequence of human sin to Him. Note well that God demands the ransom, not Satan. Sin offends God's holiness and righteousness; therefore He requires the ransom as a just payment.

For the sinner, redemption offers release from the penalty and slavery of sin (Chafer II:61). Only the Lord Jesus Christ, both God and man, could pay the great price of liberation, the price of shed blood and human life. In the context of Passover, Egypt symbolizes the sin and bondage of the world around us. The Promised Land symbolizes the release from that world.

God demonstrated the darkness of the Egyptian religion by judging its gods. He allowed Egypt to reach world-power status and acquire enormous national wealth. The combination of material wealth and total spiritual darkness forever exemplifies the darkness of the world system as described by Paul in 2 Corinthians 4:1-6. Passover pictures the Believer's redemption from the world, symbolized by Egypt, into the glorious, eternal, and personal kingdom of Jesus Christ. Chafer well summarizes both Passover and its doctrinal significance by defining redemption.

> The doctrine of redemption depicts the full payment for all sin accomplished by the death of Christ so that one who formerly was a slave to sin and subject to the righteous judgment of God is set free to serve the Lord voluntarily in a gracious relationship.
>
> (Chafer II:62).

The parallel between Passover and personal redemption is exact. In calling the former Hebrews slaves "*my people*," God signifies the personal relationship brought about by the deliverance made possible by the shed blood of a substitute lamb. God's first appointment with Israel, Passover, resulted in its deliverance and redemption as a nation. At the same time, it foreshadows the ultimate delivery that God would accomplish at Calvary on a later Feast of Passover. God, now as then, meets His people at the "*door*" (Revelation 3:20) and offers them redemption.

CHAPTER 4:
THE FEAST OF UNLEAVENED BREAD

Unleavened Bread

Moses My servant is dead; now therefore arise, go over this Jordan, thou, and all this people, unto the land which I do give to them, even to the children of Israel.

Joshua 1:2

God's second historic appointment with the nation of Israel, the Feast of Unleavened Bread, immediately followed the Passover. As can be seen from the yearly calendar, Unleavened Bread follows hard upon the heels of Passover. This close proximity is not accidental. Rather, God deliberately associated the two events with specific intent. Andrew Bonar has said that "the *passover* was the *cause*, the feast of *unleavened bread* the *effects*, of their deliverance from the grasp of Egypt" (389). While God brought deliverance to Israel through the agency of the Passover, He used Unleavened Bread to develop the people into an actual nation. Much like a wise parent caring for a new baby, God immediately instructed Moses in the care of this new nation. Part of these instructions included the details of the second feast, the Feast of Unleavened Bread.

> *And on the fifteenth day of the same month is the feast of unleavened bread unto the LORD: seven days ye must eat unleavened bread. In the first day ye shall have a holy convocation: ye shall do no servile work therein. But ye shall offer an offering made by fire unto the LORD seven days: in the seventh day is a holy convocation: ye shall do no servile work therein.*
>
> Leviticus 23:6-8

Unlike the Passover which lasted but a single day, Unleavened Bread would be celebrated over a period of seven days. Lehman Strauss explains this interesting variation: "There is a vital truth in all this. Passover, was a one-day feast, and the slaying of the lamb was a single act, but these feasts of longer duration point to the outcome of the acts" (39).

In addition to its greater length, Unleavened Bread also includes two special days bracketing the event. Both the first and the last days of the feast are "Sabbaths": days during which "servile" work is forbidden. Today we translate "servile" as "labor" or "service." In other words, during the opening and closing days of the feast, everyone avoided his or her regular, daily labor.

In order to understand this feast properly, one must first understand three significant elements:

The historic events surrounding the feast
The concept of leaven
The importance of bread in the Hebrew's life

Out of these concepts, in turn, grows the theological significance of the feast. As will become apparent, the theological relevance has a wide-reaching effect not only to the Hebrew but also to the present-day Christian. Out of the Feast of Unleavened Bread grows the doctrine of sanctification. Before drawing out this vital doctrine, however, we must explore the three preliminary elements mentioned above.

Historical Events

Immediately following the Passover, God's people faced a crucial situation in Egypt. Just the night before, God had redeemed Israel from the bondage of Egyptian slavery through the shed blood of the Passover lambs. For all practical purposes, the lambs acted as **substitutes,** purchasing the life of each Israelite firstborn when the Angel of Death passed through Egypt. In one sense, therefore, the firstborns had actually died during the night of Passover. Like Isaac of Genesis 22, however, they received life anew through the blood of the substitute lambs. Since God actually passed through Egypt on the night of Passover and since He honored the sign of blood over the doors, the firstborns now owed their lives to Him. This generation of firstborns also became the first generation of the new nation. Since He had redeemed then, God now owned the future leaders of Israel.

Logically, however, Israel could not be a true nation until it left the land of Egypt and, even more importantly, left Egypt's influence. The events of the preceding night largely accomplished this purpose by changing the balance of fear. Prior to Passover, the Hebrews lived in fear of their Egyptian masters. After Passover the Egyptians feared the Hebrews. Psalm 105:38 reports that "*Egypt was glad when they* [the Hebrews] *departed: for the fear of them fell upon them.*" The reason, of course, is obvious: the death of the Egyptian firstborns.

> *And is came to pass, that at midnight the LORD smote all the first-born in the land of Egypt, from the first-born of Pharaoh that sat on his throne unto the firstborn of the captive that was in the dungeon; and all the firstborn of cattle. And Pharaoh rose up in the night, he and all his servants, and all the Egyptians; and there was a great cry in Egypt; for there was not a house where there was not one dead.*
>
> Exodus 12:29-30

For those who had obeyed the LORD by placing the blood over their doors, there was no cry of death. This final judgment, the culmination of ten total judgments, finally forced Pharaoh to submit to the will of the LORD which he did by calling Moses and driving the Hebrews out of his land.

Rise up, and get you forth from among my people, both ye and the
children of Israel; and go, serve the LORD as ye have said. . . . and
the Egyptians were urgent upon the people, that they might send
them out of the land in haste; for they said, We be all dead men.

Exodus 12:31-33

As an interesting side note, this deliverance reveals how God acts when He acts on behalf of His people. God's deliverance did not force Israel to sneak quietly out of Egypt. Rather, they exited in grand style, literally "*driven out*" of the land. Pharaoh's command did not take the form of a reluctantly given "permission" only obtained after weeks of nagging persistence on Moses' part. Not only did God secure Israel's deliverance, He brought the haughty Pharaoh to the point of **begging** Israel to leave.

A key to understanding this second appointment lies in the mental attitudes of these two groups of people. The Egyptians feared that further destruction would befall them if they retained their Hebrew slaves any longer. As the ten plagues progressed, each became more severe and personal than the previous. After the final judgment, the Egyptians feared not only the events unfolding before their eyes but also their Hebrew slaves. When the time came, they were more than willing to accept the consequences of losing their labor force.

The Hebrews also had great fear since they had been heavily persecuted and oppressed. As a result of the preceding nine judgments, Pharaoh had increased their workload and the strictness of their taskmasters. After the events of the Passover, they probably feared Egyptian reprisals for the deaths that had occurred. When they were told to leave, they probably needed no further urging. To commemorate this moment in their history, God memorialized the first day of Unleavened Bread by making it a day free from servile work, just as that first day of freedom released them from Egyptian servile work.

The Meaning of Leaven

In order to expedite the departure of their unwelcome guests, the Egyptians gave the Hebrews anything that they requested. As we learn from Exodus, the Hebrews received the "*wealth of Egypt*" in the form

44

of gold, jewels, precious fabrics, and many other commodities. Unlike the penniless slaves of the day before, the Hebrews now possessed great national wealth. This occurrence manifests the second national aspect of the Abrahamic Covenant, *"And I will bless you."* God's provision for His people began the very day of their national birth.

Unfortunately, due to their great haste, these otherwise wealthy people were not able to prepare proper food for their upcoming journey. Instead, they baked unleavened bread, bread that did not rise before baking. *"And the people took their dough before it was leavened, their kneading troughs being bound up in their clothes upon their shoulders"* (Exodus 12:34).

Leaven is another name for yeast, the microscopic plant that makes bread rise through the process of fermentation. As yeast multiplies in an oxygen-poor environment, it generates ethyl alcohol and carbon-dioxide gas. The carbon-dioxide bubbles rising through the dough give bread its sponge-like texture. The alcohol in the dough leaves the bread during the baking process. Unleavened bread differs in one critical aspect: it contains no yeast. As a result of this absence, unleavened bread looks like a modern soda cracker (minus the salt) after baking.

In the ancient world, the leaven for the next batch of bread came from a small amount of dough put aside from the previous batch. Thus leaven's effects propagate from loaf to loaf. By using unleavened bread, the Hebrews physically and symbolically freed themselves from the leaven of Egypt.

The theological significance of the matter lies in the *action* of the yeast rather than in the yeast itself. The key point to note is that given adequate time yeast permeates an *entire* batch of dough. Leaven in and of itself is not evil. Although most conservative Christians abstain from alcoholic beverages, few avoid all products of fermentation such as ordinary breads. The alcohol created by the leaven is not the issue in this picture. Rather, the Scripture uses the *spreading* action of yeast to symbolize the pervasive action of evil. S. H. Kellog explains that Scripture uses leaven as "the established symbol of moral corruption" (457) to demonstrate how hidden sin progresses to fill the life of a man or woman.

Adding a drop of ink to a glass of water may create a good parallel to this process. In a matter of minutes, the entire glass takes on the color of the ink. Paul speaks of this same process when he reminds the carnal Christians of Corinth "*a little leaven, leaveneth the whole lump*" (I Corinthians 5:6). In the case of the Corinthians, a single man's sin was in the process of leavening the entire church. Sin always grows like a cancer within the church body unless it is stopped through proper church discipline and the sinner's repentance. God's Feast of Unleavened Bread reminded the Hebrews that just as they left the physical leaven of Egypt behind, so too should they leave its moral corruption behind.

Bread

Bread made up the bulk of the Hebrews' diet (as it did for most other people in the ancient world) and therefore offered a very meaningful example to them. Throughout the Bible bread symbolizes that which meets all of man's material needs. It therefore involves the whole of a man's physical life on earth. We can see this symbolism in action through the choice of words that Christ uses in the Disciple's Prayer when He says "*Give us this day our daily bread*" (Matthew 6:11). A literal translation might actually say "*Give us this day our daily physical needs*" and be equally accurate. Although this more generalized meaning of the word "bread" may seem odd to us today, its use was common not that long ago. Indeed, a quick perusal of the literature of the past reveals many examples in which words such as "bread" and "meat" refer to food in general rather than to specific food products.

Throughout the Scriptures God uses this all-inclusive meaning of the word "*bread*" to symbolize His blessing upon His people.

> . . . *if thou shalt hearken diligently unto the voice of the* Lord *thy God, to observe and to do all his commandments which I command thee this day, that the* Lord *thy God will set thee on high above all the nations of the earth. . . . Blessed shall be thy basket and thy kneading bowl.*
>
> Deuteronomy 28:1,5

In a similar manner, God demonstrates His curse for disobedience by sending famine into the land (a lack of physical provision). During the Wilderness Wanderings, God displayed His provision for His people by providing manna, a heavenly form of bread. Taken together, the concepts of bread (physical blessing) and leaven (sin's pervasive action) demonstrate that God expected the Hebrew's entire being to be free from sin and its pervasive action in order to receive His blessing.

In addition to its value as a symbol of sinlessness, unleavened bread also signified haste. Several other Biblical examples besides that of the Exodus support this idea. In Genesis 19:3, Lot entertains two angels. Since they arrived late in the day, he served them unleavened bread. Had their visit been expected, Lot undoubtedly would have prepared the more desirable leavened bread. Similarly, as recounted in I Samuel 28:24, the Witch of Endor serves the weak and hungry King Saul unleavened bread. Since she did not have time to prepare properly for his arrival and since Saul clearly needed food immediately, the Witch resorted to this hastily prepared form of bread. In both cases the "honored guest" came unexpectedly; therefore the host prepared a hasty form of bread.

The Second Appointment

Based upon the three elements just discussed, the meaning of this feast becomes much clearer. The Exodus was a great day in the history of Israel, forever linked with Passover in the minds of the Hebrews. Moses expresses a sense of the event's significance when he writes of it in Exodus 12:41: "*And it came to pass at the end of the four hundred and thirty years, even the selfsame day it came to pass, that all the hosts of the* LORD *went out from the land of Egypt.*" On the day of the Exodus, an estimated two-million people left Egypt via Ramses and Succoth. As Exodus 13 recounts, God personally instructed Moses and the people concerning the three major commandments of this feast.

- **The people are to sanctify the firstborn (v. 2).**
- **They are to remember the day of the Exodus by eating unleavened bread for seven days (v. 6).**
- **They are to observe the feast when they enter the Promised Land (v. 5).**

When put together, these three commands form the basis for a major theological concept. Through the first commandment, God reminds the Hebrews that He could have destroyed their firstborns in

Egypt. Since He spared their lives (if they were obedient in performing the commandments of the Passover), they now belong to Him. God commanded the Hebrews to "*Sanctify unto me all the first-born, whatsoever openeth the womb among the children of Israel, both of man and of beast: it is mine*" (Exodus 13:2). The word "sanctify" acts as the keystone of this verse. In this context it means "to consecrate" or "to separate" unto God "that which belongs to the sphere of the sacred. Thus it is distinct from the common or profane" (TWOT 786). John Davis notes an important aspect of Biblical separation: "Far too often practices of consecration have emphasized the negative whereas the biblical view of consecration is both negative and positive; that is, it involves separation *from* the world and separation *unto* God" (161). In the case of the nation of Israel, they moved from the sphere of Egypt to the sphere of God. The sanctification of the firstborn, commanded as a part of this feast, served as a constant reminder to the Hebrews that they belonged to God and not to Egypt (and by extension, the world).

The second command reminded the Hebrews that they were to be free from the moral pollution (leaven) of Egypt. As already mentioned, by physically removing the leaven from their bread, the Hebrews symbolically distanced themselves from Egypt and its pagan influences. God's people were to discard Egyptian materialism and religious practices while at the same time they were to place their dependence upon Him as their sole provider. God, not Egypt, now provides the blessing.

The third commandment harks all the way back to Abraham and the covenant God established with him. Back in Genesis 12:1, God promised a "*land*" to Abraham when he commanded him to "*Get thee out of thy country, and from thy kindred, and from thy father's house, unto a land that I will show thee.*" This promise went well beyond a simple real estate transaction. Rather, it embodied God's entire plan for the future nation of Israel.

A nation requires not only people but also unity, land, laws, government, and an economic system. God's covenant with Abraham embraces all of these concepts. As a prerequisite for obtaining the benefits of these promises, however, God commanded Abraham to separate himself from his past, his family, and his country. Initially,

Abraham only fulfilled these requirements partially. While he did leave his home in Ur, he took both his father and his nephew with him. Instead of journeying to Canaan, he sojourned in the city of Haran. In like manner, Israel failed to obey God fully with regards to Egypt. Throughout its entire period of transit from Egypt to Canaan, Israel morally returned to Egypt many times. As a consequence of these lapses, God prevented Israel from entering the Promised Land until forty years after the Exodus.

After many years of wandering, Israel finally passed through the Jordan on the tenth day of the First Month (the Day of Preparation) and camped at Gilgal (Joshua 4:19). Here they circumcised all uncircumcised males and then, on the fourteenth day, they observed the memorial of Passover. Observing the first great appointment reminded them of the way in which God had met with His people and started them on their journey to the Promised Land.

When one of the Feasts spans more than one day's time, it symbolizes "an outcome of the acts" (Strauss 39). By bracketing the entire Wilderness Period with two Passovers, God reveals the outcome of the development of the nation of Israel. Those who disobediently looked back to Egypt and hindered the immediate entrance into the land forty years ago were dead. The nation now stood purified before God as He affirmed when He declared the end of the "*reproach of Egypt*" (Joshua 5:9). On the next day, Israel ate manna for the last time (v. 11). The Lord then officially declared the completion of Israel's separation from Egypt and ended the eating of wilderness food. The entry into the Promised Land would be symbolized by the next appointment in which God officially declared the nation in the land of Canaan.

The Doctrinal Teaching

R. K. Harrison once said, "The festival of unleavened bread served as a valuable annual period of instruction, reminding the Israelites of the theological issues involved in the exodus from Egypt, and also of the implications of covenant relationship" (217). Taken on a larger scale, this memorial symbolizes the very existence of man in either a leavened or an unleavened state. Just as the action of leaven symbolizes sin, the unleavened state symbolizes freedom from sin with its associated purity.

Scripture portrays the Lord Jesus Christ in just such a way. Since it does not rise like ordinary bread, the preparer normally pierces unleavened bread to assure even baking. If he bakes the bread over a grill, the bread will also assume a striped appearance. The pictorial similarity with Christ's afflictions is too obvious to ignore. Isaiah combines the physical and the symbolic qualities of unleavened bread when, writing of the Christ, he says that *"He was wounded* [NASB, pierced through] *for our transgressions, He was bruised for our iniquities, the chastisement of our peace was upon Him, and with his stripes we are healed"* (Isaiah 53:5). Peter continues the illustration when he reminds us that Christ *"bare our sins in his own body on the tree, that we, being dead to sins, should live unto righteousness: by whose stripes ye were healed"* (I Peter 2:24).

During the Last Supper, the Lord clearly alluded to the symbolism of the unleavened bread (the only type of bread used during the Passover). *"And when he had given thanks, he brake it, and said, Take, eat: this is my body, which is broken for you, this do in remembrance of me"* (1 Corinthians 11:24). Not only did the bread symbolize Christ's purity, it also signified the haste with which He would be removed from the Cross and put in the grave before the sunset that signaled the first Sabbath of the Feast of Unleavened Bread.

Despite the triumph of their release from bondage and their subsequent entrance into the Promised Land, God reminds the Hebrews that this feast is a solemn occasion. The Law requires all men to attend the feast, while at the same time it forbids all but the most necessary work on its opening and closing day. Regardless of his personal plans, this feast significantly altered the life of the average Hebrew. Besides these basic requirements, God also demanded absolute separation from any form of leaven during the seven days of the feast.

Seven days shall ye eat unleavened bread; even the first day ye shall put away leaven out of your houses: for whosoever eateth unleavened bread from the first day until the seventh day, that soul shall be cut off from Israel.

Exodus 12:15

Although cut off "has been interpreted by some to refer to violent death, premature death, or even eternal death . . . its simplest meaning seems to [refer to] . . . one who would be cut off from all of the covenant rights and privileges normally afforded an Israelite" (Davis 150). While the term does refer to physical death on some occasions, more often it refers to what today is called excommunication. In order to prevent this fate from befalling him, the conscientious Israelite removed all leaven from his home (Exodus 12:16, Leviticus 23:6, Deuteronomy 16:18). The Scriptures also warn against leaven within the borders of Israel (Exodus 13:7, Deuteronomy 16:4).

As He does with all of the Feasts, God uses Unleavened Bread as a memorial to remind His people of the history and meaning of the historical appointment that occurred on the original occasion. Hopefully, both separation and holiness result in the nation as a consequence of this "memory jogging." To further this end, fathers were expected to teach their children the history of this appointment (Exodus 13:8). The Church can draw a lesson here. Christian worship, like the Feasts, must never lose its spiritual significance. Although we should perpetuate our worship forms and ceremonies as God directs, we must never forget what those forms and ceremonies signify. "God's ordinances are to be perpetuated not only in correct form, but as representing personal experience and correct theology" (Davis 152).

Deuteronomy 16:3 further expands on the symbolism of unleavened bread by calling it *"the bread of affliction."* Affliction in this case refers back to the time of Egyptian slavery and not to the Wilderness Period. Those who would see the Wilderness Period as a time of affliction misunderstand the purpose of the forty-year wandering. This subject will be further examined during the study of the Feast of Trumpets. Just like the bitter herbs of Passover, the unleavened bread reminds the Jewish people of the affliction of their period of slavery. They can therefore see this feast as a reminder and a picture of their removal from Egypt and the successful journey to Canaan.

During the Exodus, God employed the Red Sea crossing as a rather remarkable and clearly supernatural means of separating Israel from Egypt. When Egypt trapped Israel on the shores of the Red Sea, God's miraculous parting of the waters provided the only possible means of escape; the Israelites certainly could not have ferried themselves across.

If the Hebrews had been caught, Egyptian retaliation would have been fearful. Apart from God's miraculous intervention, Israel would have certainly returned to a captivity full of harsh reprisals. Equally true, no one can escape from the world to God apart from a supernatural work. God allowed only His own people to pass the sea on dry land. He destroyed the Egyptians who had no right to enter His land with His special people. Only people set apart by God could enter the Promised Land. In the spiritual realm, only God's people may enter Heaven. Those admitted to Heaven must be free of sin's action.

Sanctification

The Bible defines sanctification as a miracle of a changed position. Just as God physically separated the Israelites from the Egyptians at the Red Sea, so too only He can sanctify people spiritually. Without sanctification, delivered people still cannot serve a holy God. The Feast of Unleavened Bread's seven-day duration symbolizes the journey to the Promised Land. Consequently, it also symbolizes the spiritual process of sanctification.

Although one must be careful when attaching significance to numbers in the Bible, the number seven in this case clearly represents completion. The fact that the feast begins and ends with a Sabbath further suggests three distinct periods to the feast. While the regulations of the feast proscribed all servile work on the first and last days, they permitted ordinary work in the intervening five-day period. So too does the Bible indicate three distinct phases to the process of sanctification:

"Sanctification -- the miracle of a changed position."
- **Positional Sanctification: the first day, a Sabbath, of the feast**
- **Progressive Sanctification: the five ordinary days of the feast**
- **Final Sanctification: the last day, a Sabbath, of the feast**

Through His shed blood, the Lord accomplishes positional sanctification in the Believer (1 Corinthians 6:11, 2 Thessalonians 2:13, 1 Peter 1:2). Hebrews 13:12 emphasizes the idea of a blood-bought sanctification: "*That He might sanctify the people with His own blood.*" Immediately following Passover, God separated the Hebrews from the Egyptians. Historically, one would say that this separation occurred almost instantly. From the Egyptians' perspective, their former slaves were dead and gone.

Doctrinally, Paul emphasizes this relationship between the new Believer and his former masters, Sin and Satan. Romans 6:1-7:6 asserts that, once sanctified, the Believer owes no obedience to his former owners, for he has "died" to them. John Murray suggests that the definitive act of sanctification unfortunately often receives less emphasis than the process of sanctification. Associating positional sanctification with the "event of death" stresses the one-time, instantaneous aspect of sanctification (Murray 277, 279). Just as the passing through the Red Sea symbolized entering the grave, so too does the action of positional sanctification symbolize the ending of the Believer's old life (Romans 7:4).

Furthermore, the death of the body is an irreversible act. Even in Christ's case, death was not reversed; resurrection restored Him to life but did not negate the death event or its necessary significance. For the true Believer "in Jesus as the Christ and as the Son of God there is the decisive and irreversible breach with the world and with its defilement and power" (Murray 283-284). Therefore, the first aspect of sanctification occurs instantaneously and as a definitive act (Hebrews 10:10-12, Acts 26:18). Grammatically, these two passages, by their use of passive verbs, reinforce this position. The Believer is a mere passive recipient of the action performed by God. Similarly, the first day of the feast (a Sabbath) demands passivity on the part of the observer.

One must never forget, however, that even though a righteous person receives instant positional sanctification, he may still commit sins (1 John 1:9). The five days between the first and last Sabbaths of the feast symbolize the span of a Believer's life with its activities and periods of spiritual growth. A relationship with God results from the initial (positional) sanctification and deepens throughout the Believer's life (progressive sanctification). The positional sanctification must occur first, however, otherwise the relationship between humanity and a holy God would be impossible. Andrew Bonar notes that "the other [Feast of Unleavened Bread] exhibits the fellowship of God, and the holiness that follows upon pardon [Passover]" (390).

During the Wilderness Period, the Hebrews saw a limited manifestation of God through the pillar of cloud and the pillar of fire

(Exodus 13:21-22). Their positional sanctification permitted a new relationship between them and their Redeemer as a result of the shed blood of the Passover lambs. Although the deliverance accomplished at Passover freed them from their old master, the Hebrews did not immediately experience major moral changes on a personal level. Similarly, the newly saved Believer does not experience instant moral changes in his life. Salvation ends his relationship with his old master and establishes a new relationship with God, but his experience cannot instantly effect major changes. Positional sanctification makes change *possible* through a changed relationship; progressive sanctification produces the moral changes that will ultimately result in a fully reconciled Edenic relationship.

In Hebrews 2:11 the writer of the book of Hebrews describes the process of progressive sanctification. During this period of time, the Holy Spirit works in the life of the Believer to bring about complete sanctification. This process involves the Believer's cooperation through his yielding to and obeying God's will. He must therefore know the Scriptures (John 17:17) and be willing to present himself as a servant to God. In the course of the Believer's new life, God's leading and his subsequent obedience inch progressive sanctification forward. What occurs invisibly in the Believer's life occurred visibly to the newly freed Hebrews: *"And the LORD was going before them . . . to lead them on their way"* (Exodus 13:21). The Wilderness Period visually demonstrates this process through the various tests that God presented to the Israelites in order to test their obedience and faith. The worship procedure of the Tabernacle and the roles played by Moses, Caleb, and Joshua also symbolize this spiritual process.

The Wilderness Period revealed to Israel that God limits final sanctification to the true Believer. The period of wandering served to purge the unbelievers from the nation and to develop the understanding of the true Believers. The five days of the feast coincide with the forty years of wandering. During this time there is no rest but rather a period of steady growth and development. Entry into the Promised Land symbolizes the final sanctification.

God will accomplish final (or perfect) sanctification of the Church-age Believers in one of two ways: at the translation (Rapture) of the Church (Murray 298) or at the *"bema"* seat judgment. At one of these times, God will separate the Believer from all sin and bring him into complete fellowship with Himself. *"Being confident of this very thing, that he which hath begun a good work in you will perform it until the day of Jesus Christ"* (Philippians 1:6). This passage seems to support the second interpretation in which shortly after the Rapture of the saints prior to the Tribulation, the judgment seat or *"bema"* will complete the glorified saint (Pentecost 220, McClain and Whitcomb 62). 1 Thessalonians 3:13 indicates that this process must be complete before Christ returns to the earth at the end of the Tribulation. *"To the end he may stablish your hearts unblameable in holiness before God, even our Father, at the coming of our Lord Jesus Christ with all his saints."*

Once he experiences final sanctification, the Believer will be like Christ, truly sinless (1 John 3:2). Furthermore, this process includes the entire body of Christ. All Believers will reach this state at the same time. God alone, not the Believer, accomplishes the final stage of the sanctification process (1 Thessalonians 5:23-24). Since the Believer performs no *"servile work,"* this stage directly corresponds to the second Sabbath of the Feast of Unleavened Bread. God uses this symbol to portray His completed work of sanctification in the life of the Believer and his entering with Him into the Promised Land. In the eternity of rest, the true Believer serves and worships God.

A final fact must be noted. The nation as a whole performs the duties of the first and last days of the feast (the Sabbaths). The individual members of the nation observe the intervening five days. God performs the acts of positional and final sanctification upon all Believers. The period of progressive sanctification, however, depends upon each individual and his response to the working of the Holy Spirit. Progressive sanctification is a unique journey for each individual Believer. When Jesus Christ indicated in Matthew 5:48 that a man must be *"perfect,"* "he was telling them that perfection is the goal of every Believer which, even though not attainable in this life, we must strive day by day to improve in practical holiness" (Strauss 43).

Spiritual sanctification offers applications to both Jewish and Gentile Believers. The celebration of the Feast of Unleavened Bread is reserved for Israel alone, for it reminds them of the nation's physical sanctification and its resulting covenantal relationship. The first day of the feast represents the nation's coming out of the world (Egypt) through the power of God. The next five days represent the developing relationship with God as the people learn how to obey and please Him. These days also represent a period of purging during which God removes unbelievers from the assembly. Finally, the last day of the feast symbolizes the entry into the Promised Land where the nation dwells with God. Thus, the Feast of Unleavened Bread memorializes the history of Israel from its birth out of slavery into its free life in the Promised Land. History teaches Israel its unique relationship with its God as well as the demands and responsibilities of its covenant relationship.

Nisan – The First Month							
14th	15th	16th	17th	18th	19th	20th	21st
Passover	1st Sabbath						2nd Sabbath
	Feast of Unleavened Bread						
	Sanctification						
Deliverance	Positional	Progressive					Final

Figure 5 – Sanctification in the Feast of Unleavened Bread

For the Church the feast pictures the spiritual journey all true Believers experience from the moment of their salvation to the final consummation when God makes them perfect.

Purge out therefore the old leaven, that ye may be a new lump, as ye are unleavened. For even Christ our passover is sanctified for us: Therefore let us keep the feast, not with old leaven, neither with the leaven of malice and wickedness; but with the unleavened bread of sincerity and truth.

1 Corinthians 5:7-8

CHAPTER 5:
THE FEAST OF FIRST FRUITS

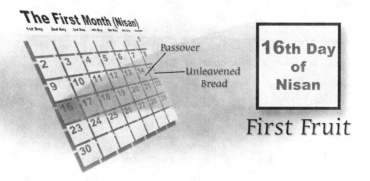

When ye be come into the land which I give unto you, and shall reap
the harvest thereof, then ye shall bring a sheaf of the first fruits . . .
Leviticus 23:10

God's third appointment, the Feast of First Fruits, is the best-defined feast in terms of history, clarity, and doctrine. In 1 Corinthians 15:20 Paul declares, *"but now is Christ risen from the dead and become the first fruits of them that slept."* The context of this verse undoubtedly implies resurrection. With the added light of the New Testament era, we, as Believers, perceive the meaning of the Feast of First Fruits with greater clarity than the Old Testament saints. For a full understanding, however, we too must study the original instructions for the feast as received by the nation of Israel.

Leviticus 23 begins the instructions for the Feast of First Fruits, as it begins the instructions for all of the other Feasts, with the phrase *"and the LORD spake unto Moses saying."*

Speak unto the children of Israel, and say unto them, When ye be come into the land which I give unto you, and shall reap the harvest thereof, then ye shall bring a sheaf of the firstfruits of your harvest unto the priest: And he shall wave the sheaf before the LORD, to be accepted for you: on the morrow after the sabbath the priest shall wave it.

Leviticus 23:10-11

While Israel first observed Passover in Egypt and fulfilled Unleavened Bread at the crossing of the Red Sea, it had to wait until it entered the Promised Land in order to celebrate First Fruits. A forty-year gap lies between the feast's institution and its first observance. Confirming that this gap was not accidental, the Scriptures predict the delay in Leviticus 23:10. First Fruits continues the symbolism developed in Passover (salvation), and Unleavened Bread (sanctification) with a new symbol: resurrection.

Why Did God Delay Entry into the Land?

In order to understand fully the meaning and ramifications of this feast, the reader must first understand God's reason for imposing the forty-year delay between the feast's institution and its observance. Three months after their deliverance and positional sanctification, God led the Israelites to Mount Sinai. Here Moses personally met with God for further instructions (Exodus 19:1-3). These instructions, known as the Mosaic Covenant, expanded the verbal covenant that God had established with Abraham, Isaac, and Jacob many years before. The Mosaic Covenant specified the laws and ordinances of the newborn nation; for all practical purposes, it acted as the nation's constitution. When Moses presented the terms of the Covenant to the people, they voiced their agreement and accepted its terms. Exodus 24:3 describes the event:

And Moses came and told the people all the words of the LORD, and all the judgments: and all the people answered with one voice, and said, All the words which the LORD hath said will we do.

Moses recorded the people's acceptance in Exodus 24:8 and sealed the Covenant by sprinkling blood upon the people. "*Behold the blood of the covenant which the Lord hath made with you concerning all these words"* (Exodus 24:8). Moses then spent forty days with God on Mount Sinai receiving additional instructions.

Unfortunately, the people's commitment to their new agreement did not last long. As the days went by and Moses' absence lengthened, the people grew restive. Instead of waiting in faith, they took matters into their own hands and acted:

> *And when the people saw that Moses delayed to come down out of the mount, the people gathered themselves together unto Aaron, and said unto him, Up, make us gods which shall go before us; for as for this Moses, the man that brought us up out of the land of Egypt, we wot not what is become of him.*
>
> Exodus 32:1

The golden calf that resulted from the people's impatience violated the first article of the new Covenant: *"I am the LORD your God, who brought you out of the land of Egypt, out of the house of bondage, Thou shalt have no other gods before me"* (Exodus 20:2-3). Interestingly, by comparing this passage to Exodus 32:1, the reader will notice that the people regarded Moses, not God, as their deliverer. Their failure to acknowledge God's role in the events of the Exodus indicates a significant spiritual deficiency on the people's part.

Within less than forty days of their original agreement to obey the LORD and follow his ordinances, the people rebelled on a national level. In righteous anger God announced His intention to destroy the people and form a new nation through Moses (Exodus 33:10). God used this situation to test Moses' qualifications as an intercessor for the nation (McClain 55). Moses passed the test and interceded for the people whom God consequently spared.

Following their initial sinful act, the nation committed nine further acts of rebellion during the transit from Mount Sinai to the borders of Canaan. Each fresh act reflected a progressively greater attitude of disobedience and discontent toward God's plan. God, in turn, recognized that the people were testing Him with each new rebellion. The tenth and final action expressed a total distrust in God's protection (Numbers 14:8-9).

The story is familiar. When the Israelites reached the borders of Canaan, Moses sent twelve spies to view the land and its people. Although the land was beautiful and fruitful, it also contained powerful inhabitants. Lacking faith in God's power, ten of the twelve spies demoralized the people and incited them to rebellion against Moses (and ultimately against God). Once again, the people forget God's promises:

Behold, I send an Angel before thee, to keep thee in the way, and to bring thee into the place which I have prepared. Beware of him, and obey his voice, provoke him not; for he will not pardon your transgressions; for my name is in him.

Exodus 23:20-21

Israel Tempts God			
Because all those men which have seen My glory, and My miracles which I did in Egypt and in the wilderness, and have tempted Me now these ten times, and have not hearkened to My voice Numbers 14:22			
Testing	Reference	Denial of God's	Location
1	Exodus 14:11,12	Sovereignty	Red Sea
2	Exodus 15:23,24	Protection	Marah
3	Exodus 16:2	Provision	Wilderness of Sin
4	Exodus 16:27	Wisdom	Kadesh
5	Exodus 17:1-3,7	Guidance	Rephidim
6	Exodus 32:1	Uniqueness	Horeb
7	Numbers 11:1	Understanding	Taberah
8	Numbers 11:4	Sufficiency	"Graves of Lust"
9	Numbers 12:1	Leadership	Hazeroth
10	Numbers 14:2	Trustworthiness	Kadesh Wilderness of Paran

Figure 6 – The Ten Tests of Numbers 14:22

God's plan for the conquest of Canaan reflects careful design and loving care for His people. Exodus 23:29-30 shows God's thoroughness as He explains how the people will conquer the land:

I will not drive them [the Canaanites] *out before you in a single year, that the land may become desolate, and the beasts of the field become too numerous for you. I will drive them out before you little by little, until you become fruitful and take possession of the land.*

Instead of relying on God's obviously superior planning, the people relied upon their own judgment. Having concluded that they could not conquer Canaan, they planned to return to Egypt and slavery. God's responded swiftly and decisively to this overt insult to His goodness and protectiveness:

Because all those men which have seen my glory, and my miracles, which I did in Egypt and in the wilderness, and have tempted [tested] *me now these ten times, and have not hearkened to my voice; Surely they shall not see the land which I sware unto their fathers, neither shall any of them that provoketh me see it:*
Numbers 14:22-23

Note a few important points here. First of all, God did not irrevocably judge His people until they had committed **ten** acts of rebellion. Such forbearance clearly demonstrates His mercy and patience toward the sinning nation. Second, note that, in reality, God did not require Israel to make an enormous leap of faith. Unlike today in which He expects the Church to walk by faith and not by sight, God gave Israel many visible proofs of His power. The same people who rejected God after hearing the spies' report had also seen Him manifest His power many times. They had seen Moses' miracles and God's judgments in Egypt. They had seen the parting of the Red Sea and the consequent destruction of their Egyptian pursuers. Finally, they had benefited from God's miraculous provision throughout their entire journey. The very manna that they ate every day attested to God's power and provision. In light of this long train of visible proofs, their rejection seems all the stranger. Since sin lives within us all, however, we should refrain from boasting in our own righteousness.

In a parallel situation to that of the Egyptians, God's people tested the LORD **ten** times. In each case the respective nations failed to acknowledge God's supremacy. The Egyptians lost their workforce and their firstborns. The mature generation of Israel lost the right to enter the Promised Land and earned the penalty of dying in the Wilderness. Once again, however, God showed mercy and justice. Although He destroyed the entire adult generation, God allowed the two righteous spies, Caleb and Joshua, and all the minority of Israel (those under twenty years of age) to enter the land.

The Entry into the Land

The next thirty-eight years of wandering served the dual purpose of purging the nation of its unbelievers and developing the fear of the LORD in its upcoming generation. Only those who truly trusted God experienced the resurrection of First Fruits. God commanded the Israelites to celebrate the feast *"on the morrow after the sabbath"* (Leviticus 23:11b), the Sabbath being the first Sabbath of the Feast of Unleavened Bread [see *Figure 7*].

Some Jewish sects and a few modern writers hold that the Sabbath in question is not any particular Sabbath but simply the last day of the week. On the other hand, orthodox Jews and most modern commentators believe that Sabbath refers to the **specific** Sabbath that opens the Feast of Unleavened Bread (Wenham 304). A careful study of the timing instructions for the Feasts substantiates the latter position. In five cases God stipulates an exact date (i.e. a particular day of the month) for the feast's observance. On the other hand, He seems to date First Fruits and Pentecost relative to the specified dates of nearby feasts. If we accept this interpretation, all of the Feasts have *exact* dates within the calendar year, not just specific days of the week. This consistent approach harmonizes best with God's revealed nature. As the reader will observe, the first three feasts cluster together and, in some cases, overlap. *Figure 7* shows the relationship between Passover, Unleavened Bread, and First Fruits.

Day of the First Month [Nisan]							
14th	15th	16th	17th	18th	19th	20th	21st
Passover							
	Sabbath						Sabbath
	Unleavened Bread						
		First Fruit					

Figure 7 – Relationship of First Three Feasts

The Scriptures stipulate two prerequisites that the Israelites had to fulfill before they could observe the Feast of First Fruits. First, the nation had to be in the Promised Land. Second, the feast had to occur at harvest time. God demonstrated His sovereignty over times and events by bringing Israel into the land at precisely the right time. At the conclusion of the forty years of wandering, God tells Joshua, *"Moses my servant is dead; now therefore arise, go over this Jordan, thou, and all this people, unto the land which I do give to them, even to the children of Israel"* (Joshua 1:2). The time had come for the purged nation to enter its future land. God, in His providence, brought the nation to Canaan during the spring harvest. *"And the people came up out of Jordan on the tenth day of the first month, and encamped in Gilgal, in the east border of Jericho"* (Joshua 4:19).

Forty years earlier, the Hebrews had prepared for the upcoming Passover that would deliver them from Egypt. Once again, they prepared to celebrate this time of remembrance: *"And the children of Israel encamped in Gilgal, and kept the passover on the fourteenth day of the month at even in the plains of Jericho"* (Joshua 5:10). The next day they ate manna for the last time as they began the first Sabbath of the Feast of Unleavened Bread (Joshua 5:11-12). Later, they would eat the produce of the land.

Before they celebrated the feasts, however, they restored a lapse in their covenant relationship with God. Since the nation had neglected the rite of circumcision during its forty-year period in the Wilderness, Joshua circumcised all of the sons of Israel (Joshua 5:2) before they observed the feasts. Through this action, the nation reaffirmed its covenant with God. Only in a covenant relationship could Israel celebrate the Feasts.

Camped within the Promised Land, Israel first observed the Passover followed by the first day of Unleavened Bread. Then, for the first time in their history, the Hebrews celebrated the Feast of First Fruits. The first fruits came from their new land, the land of Canaan. *"But they did eat of the fruit of the land of Canaan that year"* (Joshua 5:12).

By bringing His people into the land during the First Month, its most fruitful period, God demonstrates His abundant provision for His own people. Although they did not know it, the Canaanites had planted, cultivated, and prepared a harvest for God's people to reap. Since the harvest time lasted for six months, God saw to it that His people had food throughout the early days of the Conquest. God's timing shows that His plans are always best.

In offering God the first fruits of the land, the people "look[ed] forward to the sedentary occupation of Canaan" (Harrison 217). The Hebrew people would now become an agricultural society instead of a band of wandering nomads. They would depend upon the LORD for their future harvests and national prosperity. The offering of the first fruits of the harvest reflects their dependence upon God for their well-being as a nation (Bonar 392).

Unlike pagan "first fruits" rituals, Israel's Feasts were not "the recognition of the fruitful life of nature . . . but of Jehovah, as the Author and Sustainer of the life of His covenant people Israel." Pagan feasts celebrated the ruling influence of nature on life and the harvest. Israel, by contrast, recognized their unique covenant relationship with God which required total obedience to His will as well as a recognition of that will (Kellogg 432).

Christ's Resurrection on the Feast of First Fruits

Often in history God uses one historic event to prefigure a greater event. The first event, therefore, serves as a picture of the more significant future event. First Fruits performs just such a role. The original pictorial event began in the Wilderness and culminated in failure when the spies returned with a negative report. Its joyful consummation, delayed by the nation's sin, finally occurred thirty-eight years later when the nation entered the Promised Land.

The second, more significant event occurred in 30 AD on the tenth day of the First Month. On this day the Scriptures commanded the nation of Israel to select a perfect lamb for the upcoming annual Passover. On this day Jesus Christ entered Jerusalem offering Himself in peace as the King of Israel. The crowds that gathered to meet Him proclaimed Him the "*King of Israel that cometh in the name of the Lord*" (John 12:13). Unfortunately, the people were not looking for a spiritual Messiah Who would save them from their sins. Instead they hoped that Jesus would deliver them from the political bondage of Rome.

Just four days later on Passover, the same crowd that had acclaimed Him king, turned upon Him and demanded His crucifixion. During the fifteenth of the month, the first Sabbath of Unleavened Bread, His sinless (unleavened) body remained in the tomb. On the sixteenth of the month, the Feast of First Fruits, Christ arose from the dead. Paul unquestionably refers to this event and to the day on which it occurred when he declares Christ the "*first fruit of them that slept*" (2 Corinthians 15:20). Obviously, God ordained this sequence of three feasts as a part of Israel's national history. In light of the New Testament, however, it becomes equally clear that God also ordained it as a picture of a far greater spiritual event that would ultimately benefit all of mankind. *Figure 8* shows the first three feasts along with their national and spiritual significances.

In each case the first historical event applied to the nation of Israel. The second historical event for each of these feasts affected not only the nation of Israel but went well beyond it to include all of mankind. Looking at the complete picture with New Testament eyes, we can see that the original historical event served as a picture that foretold the upcoming, broader spiritual truth. Lehman Strauss explains:

> Our study to this point has brought to light the fact that these Old Testament feasts are not restricted to national Israel. When the Scriptures of the Old and New Testaments are studied together, it becomes clear that there is a wider message of prophecy and salvation for both Jew and Gentile.

He also emphasizes the fact that these feasts "present God's prophetic calendar pointing to their wider fulfillment in the Lord Jesus Christ. The holy days in the calendar . . . are a shadow of things to come; but the body is of Christ" (Strauss 55).

The Doctrinal Teaching

These great historical events in the nation of Israel serve to clarify further the doctrines of God, both those that apply to the Feasts and those that more widely apply to the saints of all ages. By allowing Israel to enter the Promised Land on the anniversary of its deliverance from Egypt, God ties deliverance, sanctification, and first fruits together. In the same way, these three feasts coincide with the Lord's death, burial, and resurrection. Through these three events, God fulfills the covenant promise that He gave to Abraham, a blessing for all the families of the earth (Genesis 12:3).

To understand the doctrinal background for the Feast of First Fruits, we must first understand the term "first fruits" from an etymological standpoint. The root word for "first" may be translated "beginning" or "best." This same word form appears over fifty times in the Old Testament and usually refers to the "first or beginning of a series" or "the choicest or best of a group or class of things, particularly in reference to items to be set aside for God's service or sacrifices" (TWOT 825). Leviticus 2:12 and 23:10, Nehemiah 12:44, and Numbers 18:12 all contain examples of this usage. God uses this very form in the first words of Genesis *"In the beginning"* to suggest that the first event of Creation was the first in a series of such events.

Significance of the First Three Feasts of the Lord				
Historical Timing	**Applied to**	**Passover**	**Unleavened Bread**	**First Fruits**
Old Testament	**Israel**	**In Egypt**	**Separated from Egypt**	**First Blessing of Promised Land**
New Testament	**Mankind**	**The Cross**	**Spiritual Separation**	**Christ arose First of many to come**
Doctrine ->		**Redemption**	**Separation**	**Resurrection**

Figure 8– Significance of the First Three Feasts of the Lord

Three major teachings emerge from this feast. First, the Feast of First Fruits demonstrates God's provision for His people, Israel, when they entered the land. God never intended this feast as a fertility or supplication rite. Pagan cultures observed harvest feasts in order to placate their gods in the hopes of a good harvest. Israel, on the other hand, gave thanks to God through its feast. The Feast of First Fruits memorializes an **event** that occurred at a particular harvest (the entry into the Promised Land); it did not function as an agricultural or fertility feast (Bush 236).

Second, God expanded the purpose of the feast after the Israelites entered the land. In addition to commemorating a specific historical moment, God also uses the feast as a means by which Israel could thank Him for His provision and acknowledge His supremacy over all. God asked Israel to give back the "best" as an acknowledgment of His ownership. "One reason why God gave the land of Canaan to Israel was to give to the people something they could give back to Him" (Strauss 60). In effect, God stands as the landlord of the universe with humans as His tenants. Israel's covenant with God functions as a kind of lease. Such a perspective explains why God could evict His people from the land and then later restore them; if they violate the terms of the lease (covenant), the landlord takes the actions specified in the lease.

Third, the feast looks to the future with the "best" being a representative of good things to come. In a purely physical context, the first fruits of the harvest symbolize the upcoming crops that waited harvesting in the fields. In the spiritual realm, Christ's resurrection symbolizes the first fruits of resurrection. A whole harvest of resurrected Believers will someday follow Christ as a result.

Although our English Bible does not readily reveal it, God makes an interesting point through the use of two distinct Hebrew words when He gives the instructions for the Feast of First Fruits (Leviticus 23:9-22). Verse 10 states: "*Speak unto the children of Israel, and say unto them, When ye be come into the land which I give unto you, and shall reap the harvest thereof, then ye shall bring a sheaf of the first fruits of your harvest unto the priest.*" Verse 17 indicates: "*Ye shall bring out of your habitations two wave loaves of two tenth deals: they shall be of fine flour; they shall be baked with leaven; they are the first fruits unto the LORD.*" As the reader will notice, the translators of the Authorized Version use the same expression in each verse. In the original Hebrew, however, these two verses employ entirely different words. The original word used in Verse 10 should actually be translated "firstlings" instead of "first fruits." The translators' choice used in verse 17 is acceptable as it stands. By using two different Hebrew words, God conveys two important aspects to the feast that our English Bible unfortunately conceals.

The first form ("firstlings") serves to remind the Hebrews that their firstborns belong to God. By sparing the firstborns when He passed through Egypt, God purchased them and thus became their owner. Numbers 8:17 supports this interpretation: "*For all the firstborn of the children of Israel are mine, both man and beast: on the day that I smote every firstborn in the land of Egypt I sanctified them for myself.*"

The second word form ("first fruits") reminds the people that their harvest comes from God. As a consequence, they must be grateful to Him and acknowledge His role in providing the harvest.

First and foremost, First Fruits teaches the Israelite that he must meet with his God every year to honor Him for His provision in the Promised Land. The harvest came as a result of his presence in the land that God gave him. The first harvest along with its successors reflects God's covenantal care for His people in providing them with the land in which they live. The feast, therefore, focuses on the covenant relationship. As long as they were in the land, the harvests would follow. Andrew Bonar sees the first historical First Fruits as God's "pledge and earnest of all the harvests" (393). In a sense the future harvests would serve as an indicator of the nation's status in its covenantal relationship with its God.

The physical specifications of the feast also serve to demonstrate and acknowledge God's covenantal care. During the worship service on the day of the feast, the priest took a sheaf of barley gathered at the beginning of the harvest and "waved" it before the LORD (Leviticus 23:11). He held the sheaf in front of him, lifted it above his head, dropped it towards his waist, and finally moved it to the left and to the right. Harrison points out that this motion forms the shape of a cross thus typifying Christ's future role in connection with the feast (217). The movement also symbolizes the fact that the sheaf was just the beginning of a harvest that had obtained its "life" from God.

When the priest accepted the first yield from the harvest, he said to the bearer, "*I profess this day to the LORD thy God that I am come unto the country which the LORD sware unto our fathers for to give us*" (Deuteronomy 26:10). Notice that this statement clearly demonstrates the recognition of God's role in the land and in the Covenant. It recalls the new life (v. 9) in the Promised Land made possible by God's redemption (vv. 5-7) and sanctification (v. 8). "When Israel tasted the barley of Canaan, then were they fully sensible of completed deliverance from Egypt and the desert" (Bonar 394). God instituted the feast as a perpetual ordinance for the nation; the Israelites were to celebrate it each year of the nation's existence.

Just as barley, the first yield of the harvest, symbolizes all that follows, so Jesus Christ symbolizes the first yield of the resurrection of true Believers. "*But every man in his own order, Christ the first fruits; afterward they that are Christ's at his coming*" (1 Corinthians 15:23). Wheat and then fruits follow barley in Israel's harvest sequence. So too, in the spiritual realm, each harvest of souls comes in "order." Much like a procession, many other souls will follow Christ.

God further reinforces this harvest metaphor in 1 Corinthians 15:35-38. Here He compares the resurrected body to a seed that dies when it is sown but then comes to life again as it grows. "*How are the dead raised up? . . . that which thou sowest is not quickened* [made alive], *except it die.*" Jesus Christ was the first of a series of resurrected souls, each of which is buried and set apart from the world prior to resurrection. The future resurrection will follow a precise order.

First, the New Testament saints (alive and dead) will be raised (1 Thessalonians 4:13-18). During the Tribulation the two martyrs will follow (Revelation 11:11-12). At the Second Coming at the conclusion of the Tribulation, the Old Testament saints and the Tribulation martyrs will take their place (Daniel 12:1-2, Revelation 7:14, 20:4). Finally, the unsaved will be resurrected for their ultimate judgment in the Lake of Fire (Revelation 20:11-14). Although all mankind will experience a resurrection, not all will receive fellowship with God; on the contrary, for many, resurrection leads to judgment and final, eternal separation from God.

In addition to the simple order that they suggest, the various crops of Israel's harvest also symbolize the various groups of people saved throughout the ages. Barley, the first crop, symbolizes those saved from the nation of Israel. Paul states, "*For I am not ashamed of the gospel of Christ, for it is the power of God unto salvation, to every one that believeth, to the Jew first, and also to the Greek*" (Romans 1:16). Since Israel nationally rejected the LORD, He temporarily put them aside on a national basis (but **not** on an individual basis). Paul reminds all men that Israel's rejection serves a function to the rest of mankind: "*For if the casting away of them be the reconciling of the world, what shall the receiving of them be, but life from the dead? For if the firstfruit be holy: and if the root by holy, so are the branches*" (Romans 11:15-16).

After the harvest of Israel (barley), the wheat harvest of individual Jewish people and the Gentile nations begins. This harvest will include people from all parts of the earth. The Bible lists a few of the "first fruits" of the Gentile nations including Epaenetus of Asia (Romans 16:15) and the household of Stephanus in Achaia (1 Corinthians 16:15). In its almost two thousand year history, the Church has spread over the entire earth.

At the completion of the wheat harvest (individual Jews and Gentiles), a dispersed Israel will experience a national re-awakening and recognize Jesus Christ as the true Messiah. The final "crop" of 144,000 Jewish people along with their converts, analogous to the fruit harvest at the end of the Jewish agricultural cycle, will be harvested during the

Tribulation. "*These were redeemed from among men, being the first fruits unto God and to the Lamb*" (Revelation 14:4).

Christ, as the first fruits of a new resurrection, marks the beginning of the many who will come to know the Him and will be His spiritual harvest. The nationalities and circumstances may vary, but God will call forth His people and bring them to new life in His Promised Land of Heaven. The Feast of First Fruits, an appointment with God for Israel, vividly pictures God's larger plan of resurrection for all of those who believe.

Modern Israel no longer remembers or observes the Feast of First Fruits. Temporarily, they are out of their covenant relationship with their God. As it will be with the other feasts, however, Israel will someday celebrate the Feast of First Fruits in the Millennial kingdom of Jesus Christ. When this time comes, they will celebrate the feast as a time of remembrance of the new resurrected life made possible by the resurrection of that First Fruit, the Lord Jesus Christ.

CHAPTER 6:
PENTECOST

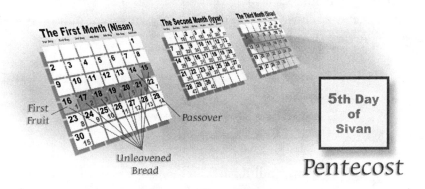

Ye shall bring out of your habitations two wave loaves of two tenth deals: they shall be of fine flour; they shall be baked with leaven; they are the first fruits unto the LORD.

Leviticus 23:17

The first three feasts of Leviticus 23 each tie in to a specific historical event in the history of the nation of Israel. Like the first three feasts, the fourth appointment, the Feast of Pentecost, shows another such link. Scripture associates Pentecost with a number of significant events: the Exodus with its accompanying Wilderness Period experience, the founding of the Mosaic Covenant, and the first seasonal harvest crop. In order to understand the spiritual significance of the Feast of Pentecost, we must again first examine the historical events connected with the feast.

Historical Initiation of the Feast: The Covenant Ratified

The people of Israel left the land of Goshen on the fifteenth day of the First Month (Numbers 33:3). After crossing the Red Sea, they made stops in Marah, Elim, Dophkah, Alush, and finally Rephidim. Precisely one month after the start of the Exodus, on the fifteenth day of the Second Month, they arrived at the Wilderness of Sin (Exodus 16:1). In the Third Month, Israel reached Mt. Sinai and kept its second divine meeting with its Redeemer, the LORD.

As Israel camped at the foot of Mt. Sinai, God gave Moses the instructions for the covenant that would eventually be known as the Mosaic or Sinaitic Covenant (Exodus 19:2). The Mosaic Covenant, Israel's national constitution, contains three important promises for the young nation (Exodus 19:5-6).

- **Israel would be God's chosen people among all the nations of the world.**
- **Israel would be a kingdom of priests to Him.**
- **Israel would be a holy nation.**

Unlike the unconditional Abrahamic Covenant, the Mosaic Covenant indicated that the nation's actions determined God's responses. If the nation obeyed the LORD, He would bless them. If they disobeyed Him, cursing and chastisement would follow. Note that the covenant relationship depended upon the **nation's** actions rather than those of individuals. Individuals might break the conditions of the Mosaic Covenant without hurting the nation as a whole (although in other situations the actions of individuals certainly **did** hurt the nation as a whole). Israel's physical presence in the land along with its observance of the Feasts would indicate God's blessing, while dispersion (exile) with the accompanying termination of the Feasts would indicate His curse (Leviticus 26). God would tangibly show His displeasure through this mode of chastisement.

> *And He* [God] *hath violently taken away his tabernacle, as if it were of a garden; He hath destroyed His places of the assembly: the*

> LORD *hath caused the solemn feasts and Sabbaths to be forgotten in Zion.*
>
> Lamentations 2:6

When Moses presented the basic terms of the constitution (the Covenant) at Mt. Sinai, the people gave their unqualified acceptance (Exodus 19:8). Following their verbal affirmation a process of preparing, reviewing, accepting, and ratifying the Covenant occurred. In the middle of this critical time in Israel's national history, God came

> *. . . down in the sight of all the people upon mount Sinai . . . in the morning . . . there were thunders and lightnings, and a thick cloud upon the mount, and the voice of the trumpet exceeding loud; so that all the people that was in the camp trembled.*
>
> Exodus 19:11-16

Moses and the people had just met their covenant God, the King of kings and Lord of lords.

At the end of these days of instruction, terror, and awe, the nation formally accepted the Covenant and ratified it with blood. Thus, in the Third Month, Israel officially became a nation governed by constitutional law (Exodus 24:4-8).

Establishing the Day of Ratification

A great deal of scholarly debate centers upon the determination of the actual day on which the nation ratified the Covenant. Exodus 19:1 provides key dating information: "*In the third month, when the children of Israel were gone forth out of the land of Egypt, the same day* [on that very day – NASB] *came they into the wilderness of Sinai.*" Much hinges upon the phrase, "*on that very day.*" Some scholars believe "the best interpretation of this Hebrew expression . . . is simply 'at this time'" (Davis 202, Keil 89). Others, however, take a more literal approach to the passage and hold that "*on that very day*" refers to the first day of the Third Month. The Feast of Pentecost, which comes fifty days after the Feast of First Fruits, also falls in the Third Month, the month during which the nation ratified the Covenant. Many therefore connect the events of Exodus 24 with this feast. If Exodus 19:1 **does** refer to the first day of the month, then we can link the events of Exodus 19:24 to the Feast of Pentecost. Since the simplest and most direct interpretation of the passage favors this conclusion, we accept it and treat the two events as intentionally linked together by God.

The Sequence of Events

On the first day of the Third Month, the day that the Hebrews reached Mt. Sinai, Moses ascended the mountain and briefly met with God. He then returned (Exodus 19:3-7) to the people and reminded them that their God controls all events. *"Ye have seen what I did unto the Egyptians, and how I bare you on eagles' wings, and brought you unto myself"* (Exodus 19:4). Moses then enumerated the three promises that the LORD made to the nation (the three listed at the beginning of this chapter). Fulfillment of these promises depended upon the nation's obedience and God's timing.

Exodus 19:8 records that Israel verbally accepted these promises and the conditions required for their fulfillment. Having received the nation's promise, Moses returned to the mountain and met with the LORD for further instructions. The LORD then told the people to consecrate (sanctify) themselves for two days in preparation to meet with Him. Thus, Day 1 of the Third Month included discussions, verbal acceptance, instructions, and the first day of cleansing, while Day 2 continued the cleansing and preparation process. On Day 3 (Exodus 19:11) Israel met its God (Exodus 19:17-20) and heard the preamble of the Covenant, the Ten Commandments (Exodus 20:1-17). Moses also received additional instruction about the future Law (Exodus 20:23-23:33). The people then verbally accepted the preamble (Exodus 24:3), their **second** verbal acceptance of the Covenant.

From this point on, the chronology of the succeeding events becomes a bit more complicated necessitating a very careful analysis of chapters 19 through 24. *Figure 9* shows the simplest chronology that accounts for the events and harmonizes with the passages. Four distinct days form the basis of this chronology. These include the two days that involved instruction, the people's first verbal acceptance, and the time of preparation followed by the formal meeting with God on the third day during which Moses presented the Ten Commandments, received the basic tenets of the Law, and received the people's second verbal acceptance. The Scriptures clearly indicate that the first three days are sequential. The fourth day, unfortunately, is more problematic and requires us to make certain deductions about its relationship to the other three since the Scriptures do not explicitly state its position in time,

Proposed Sequence of Events in the Third Month at Mt. Horeb					
Third Month Sivan	1st Day	2nd Day	3rd Day	4th Day	5th Day
Events of the Day	First acceptance by people ——— Moses returns to God ——— 1st Day of Preparation	2nd Day of Preparation	Second acceptance by people ——— Moses read the Preamble ——— Moses goes to Meet with God	Moses wrote the words of the LORD	Third acceptance by people ——— Covenant formally ratified and sealed with blood
Reference	Exodus 19:10		Exodus 19:16, 17	Exodus 24:4a	Exodus 24:4b, 7, 8

Figure 9 – Events at Mt. Horeb

We learn from Exodus 24:4-8 that after he presented the preamble and received the people's second verbal acceptance on the third day, Moses then

> *wrote all the words of the LORD, and rose up early in the morning, and builded an altar under the hill, . . . and he took the book of the covenant, and read in the audience of the people: and they said, All that the LORD hath said will we do, and be obedient. And Moses*

took the blood, and sprinkled it on the people, and said, Behold the blood of the covenant, which the LORD hath made with you concerning all these words.

Exodus 24:4-8

The passage seems to imply the presence of an **additional** day separating the events of the third day from the formal blood ratification of the Covenant on the final or fifth day. Exodus 24:4 tells us that Moses rose early after he *"wrote all the words of the LORD."* Logic leads us to conclude that Moses spent the fourth day recording the words of the LORD (Exodus 24:4a) recounted in Exodus 20:23-23:33 and then rose early on the fifth day (Exodus 24:4b) to perform the formal ratification of the Covenant.

Exodus 24:7 tells us that Moses read a *"book"* before the people after which they affirmed their obedience to its contents. Following their acceptance of the Covenant (their **third** acceptance), Moses sprinkled the people with the *"blood of the covenant"* (Exodus 24:8) signifying their formal ratification of the Covenant and its terms and conditions.

We can also presume that the *"book"* referred to in Exodus 24:7 contained only the preamble (Exodus 20:1-17) and the basic terms of the Law (Exodus 20:23-23:33) at this point since we know that God gave the remainder of the Covenant to Moses during the later forty-day period that he spent on the mountain (Exodus 25-31). We therefore conclude that on Day 4 Moses recorded the words of the LORD and that the formal blood ratification occurred on Day 5. There were thus **five** eventful days before Moses departed for his forty days upon the mountain with God. Since this five-day period commenced on the first of the month, we can safely conclude that the blood ratification occurred on the fifth day of the Third Month. Since the fifth day of the Third Month comes exactly fifty days after the Feast of First Fruits, we can also conclude that Day 5, the day of ratification, coincides with the Feast of Pentecost.

Both tradition and scholarly research support this position. "According to unanimous Jewish tradition, which was universally received at the time of Christ, the day of Pentecost was the anniversary of the giving of the Law on Mount Sinai, which the Feast of Weeks [another name for Pentecost] was intended to commemorate" (Edersheim 260). Maimonides affirms the notion that the Law was given at Pentecost (Lange 176) as does Victor Buksbazen who, basing his conclusions upon ancient rabbinical calculations, claims that this feast first occurred at the giving of the Law. He states, "Being the anniversary of the giving of the Law on Mount Sinai, Pentecost is considered as the birthday of Judaism" (16). Modern Jewish teaching unites Pentecost with the giving of the Law as the "unique spiritual experience that indelibly stamped the Israelites with their unique character, their faith, and their destiny" (Donin 239).

While we cannot dogmatically state that the ratification of the Covenant coincided with Pentecost, *Figures 9* shows that Pentecost must have occurred within one day of that event. This proximity may explain why the translators of the Authorized and the New American Standard translations chose "*the same day*" or "*on that very day*" as appropriate, instead of "at this time." The specificity of this phrase linked with the Third Month strongly suggests the connection between the two events. Since no other major national event so closely coincides with Pentecost, we hold that the Feast of Pentecost memorializes the day on which the nation of Israel ratified its Covenant, the "birth" of Judaism.

Linking to Pentecost

If the birth of Judaism coincides with the Feast of Pentecost, then a unique linkage also exists with the Pentecost of Acts 2. Long taught as the birth of the Church, the Pentecost of Acts 2 now expands in importance as a result of its connection to the birth of the nation of Israel. Further, such a linkage shows that Pentecost also symbolizes God's temporary suspension of the Mosaic Covenant relationship with Israel.

In an amazingly short time after its ratification of the Covenant, the nation quickly sinned breaking it through their construction and worship of the golden calf. Speaking of the people, God relates that

> *They have turned aside quickly out of the way which I commanded them . . . and the* Lord *said unto Moses, I have seen this people, and behold, it is a stiff necked people: Now therefore let me alone,*

81

that my wrath may wax hot against them, and that I may consume
them: and I will make of thee a great nation.

Exodus 32:8-10

Moses argues with God against His decision to destroy the newly born nation. In verse 11, Moses reminds God that it was He Who brought them out *"with great power and with a mighty hand."* Moses contends that if God were to destroy them, the other nations would believe that God's purposes were malignant at heart. This perception, Moses says, would tarnish God's integrity. Further, since God had promised Abraham, Isaac, and Jacob (Exodus 32:13) unconditional faithfulness to their descendants, a righteous God would never go back upon His word. After testing Moses through these arguments, God relents and Moses returns to the camp to deal with the sinning nation.

Upon seeing the golden calf and the pagan dancing, Moses becomes equally incensed at the people and breaks the tablets of the Law thereby symbolizing the broken Covenant (Exodus 32:19). Moses, following the Scriptural instructions of Numbers 5:11-22, then performs the test for adultery upon the people (Exodus 32:20). He asks, *"Who is on the LORD's side? Let him come unto me"* (Exodus 32:26). The sons of Levi respond and, following Moses' instructions for the adultery test, determine that three thousand people are guilty of spiritual adultery. They then separate these adulterous people from the Covenant and destroy them.

Moses attempts to atone for the people in much the same way as Paul wishes to do for Israel in Romans 9:3. God indicates that on a future day He would punish the nation for its sin of adultery: *"Therefore now go, lead the people unto the place of which I have spoken unto thee: behold, mine angel shall go before thee: nevertheless in the day when I visit I will visit their sin upon them"* (Exodus 32:34). That day of punishment would come at Kadesh as Numbers 14:26 records (Keil 232). Through this incident, we learn something of God's nature; He is a *"jealous God"* (Exodus 34:14). The first breaking of the Covenant resulted in the physical death of three thousand people from the nation of Israel.

Beginning with the first historical Pentecost, Israel would celebrate the feast as a memorial to remind them of the Law that God gave them at Mount Sinai. The modern Jewish explanation for this feast emphasizes its spiritual significance. Shavuot mentions the spiritual lesson that the release from bondage and the winning of political freedom do not constitute complete freedom unless they culminate in the spiritual restraints, disciplines, and duties inherent in the Revelation to Israel and in Israel's acceptance of the Torah (Keil 240).

The Instructions for the Feast of Pentecost

The Scriptures link the Feast of Pentecost, much as they link the Feast of First Fruits, to the harvest. Exodus 23:16 calls Pentecost the Feast of Harvest. It is also variously known as the Day of Pentecost, the Day of the First Fruit (Keil 240), the Feast of the Fiftieth Day, and the Feast of Weeks (Exodus 34:22, Deuteronomy 16:10, 16, 2 Chronicles 8:13) (Edersheim 262). Leviticus 23:15-22 gives the instructions for the feast:

> *And ye shall count unto you from the morrow after the sabbath, from the day that ye brought the sheaf of the wave offering; seven sabbaths shall be complete: Even unto the morrow after the seventh sabbath shall ye number fifty days; and ye shall offer a new meat offering unto the LORD. Ye shall bring out of your habitations two wave loaves of two tenth deals: they shall be of fine flour; they shall be baked with leaven; they are the firstfruits unto the LORD. And ye shall offer with the bread seven lambs without blemish of the first year, and one young bullock, and two rams: they shall be for a burnt offering unto the LORD, with their meat offering, and their drink offerings, even an offering made by fire, of sweet savour unto the LORD. Then ye shall sacrifice one kid of the goats for a sin offering, and two lambs of the first year for a sacrifice of peace offerings. And the priest shall wave them with the bread of the firstfruits for a wave offering before the LORD, with the two lambs: they shall be holy to the LORD for the priest. And ye shall proclaim on the selfsame day, that it may be an holy convocation unto you: ye shall do no servile work therein: it shall be a statute for ever in all your dwellings throughout your generations. And when ye reap*

the harvest of your land, thou shalt not make clean riddance of the corners of thy field when thou reapest, neither shalt thou gather any gleaning of thy harvest: thou shalt leave them unto the poor, and to the stranger: I am the LORD your God.

Because of the number of days that separate this feast from the Feast of First Fruits, the feast was given the name of Pentecost, (Greek, *penthkosth*) which means "the fiftieth" (Hoehner 1306).

In order to understand this feast, we must first understand the relationship between the historical appointment and the harvests. Chapter 5 mentions that the first harvest begins in the First Month near the Feast of First Fruits. Farmers harvest the barley crop first. The wheat harvest, which follows the barley, begins on the fifth day of the Third Month. The Israelites considered the time of this "*new meat offering*" (AV) or "*new grain offering*" (NASB, Leviticus 23:16) as the time of the fullest harvest. Pentecost, as appointed by God, marks the juncture between the two principal crops. Leviticus 23:15-22 proclaims the beginning of the second harvest by stating that it should occur precisely seven Sabbaths after the start of the Feast of Unleavened Bread, precisely fifty days after that feast.

Seven Sabbaths suggests the idea of completion, the completion of a set period of time or of a specific harvest. Since this feast marks the end of the first harvest, it appears that the number seven does have a symbolic association with this feast in addition its literal chronological sense. This symbolism meets the criteria established by John Davis for the symbolic interpretation of numbers (see Davis 155). Additionally, the instructions for this feast again prohibit "*servile work.*" This command conveys the idea of ceasing or the cessation of some activity, in this case the barley harvest. Further, Jewish tradition designates this feast as "*hag ha Azereth*" or simply "*Azereth*" meaning the "feast of conclusion" or just "conclusion" (Edersheim 262). Leviticus 23:17 indicates that the people of Israel should treat this new crop as a "*first fruits unto the LORD,*" just as they treated the barley crop at the Feast of First Fruits.

On the Feast of Unleavened Bread, the people offer a single loaf of unleavened bread; on Pentecost they offer two loaves of leavened bread (see *Figure 10*). This difference further reinforces our earlier conclusion that yeast in and of itself is not evil; rather, leaven's pervasive **action** is its key significance. It should be further noted that of all the cereal offerings described in the Scriptures, only the fine wheat flour offering involved leaven (Buksbazen 17). For this reason, we conclude that Scripture intentionally links wheat and leaven for some spiritual purpose.

Feast of Unleavened Bread	Feast of Pentecost
1 Loaf of Unleavened Bread	2 Loaves of Leavened Bread
Exodus 12:15	Leviticus 23:17

Figure 10 – Bread offerings

Numbers 28:26 creates some initial confusion by referring to Pentecost as the Feast of First Fruits. The passage is **not** referring to *the* Feast of First Fruits that occurs during the Feast of Unleavened Bread. Instead, by using this title, Numbers emphasizes the fact that Pentecost marks the beginning of the **second** major harvest (wheat). Because the Scriptures call Pentecost **a** feast of first fruits, we can expect to see symbolism similar to that used in the Feast of First Fruits. As with the earlier feasts, the Scriptures stress the importance of observing the feast properly. These requirements specify that

No laborious work is to be performed during the feast.
All the men of Israel are to gather in Jerusalem.
It is to be a perpetual feast.

Significantly, the Scriptures extend this feast by allowing Gentiles to participate in its observance. This quality differs sharply from Passover in which the Scriptures specifically exclude Gentiles (Exodus 12:48). The "Law of the Gleanings," explained in Leviticus 23:22, sets the conditions for Gentile involvement. It was this regulation that helped Ruth, a Gentile Moabitess, to survive when she returned with Naomi to Bethlehem. In modern times, Jewish people read the book of Ruth publicly when they observe the Feast of Pentecost. Their action seems appropriate since most of the book of Ruth takes place in Bethlehem, whose name literally means "the house of bread." The historical connection also serves to remind the Jewish people that even a Gentile can come to know and love the God of Naomi (Buksbazen 18-19).

The Law of the Gleanings requires the reapers to leave the corners of the field unharvested as well as to leave the gleanings of the harvest for needy people and the strangers in the land. This practice functioned as a type of social program for the poor. In Israel, the term "stranger" (*ger*) refers to people "who live among people who are not blood relatives; thus, rather than enjoying native civil rights, the ger was dependent on the hospitality that played an important role in the ancient near east" (TWOT 150). While they lived in Egypt, the people of Israel were sojourners (*ger*) in Egypt (Genesis 15:13, Exodus 23:9). In Israel the *ger*, "largely a proselyte . . . enjoyed many of the same rights as the native and was not to be oppressed" (TWOT 156). Deuteronomy 10:18 says that the LORD loves the strangers. This subject will come up again when we explore the doctrinal teachings of this feast.

The Celebration of the Feast of Pentecost

The Feast of Pentecost is a joyous time in Israel. Farmers complete the barley harvest happy in the knowledge that more bounty lies ahead. Although Pentecost fosters great joy due to its connection with the harvest, it serves a far greater purpose than a mere thanksgiving. Pentecost also does much more than memorialize the birth of a nation. Like the earlier feasts, we find that God first directs Pentecost's purposes toward the nation of Israel. Its later significance reaches out to all mankind. This later appointment also reveals the critical relationship between Israel and the Church.

Scriptural commandment requires all men to return to Jerusalem since Pentecost is the second Pilgrimage Feast or *hag* (Exodus 23:14, 17). Psalm 120-134 record the spiritual hymns sung on these occasions. Due to its mountaintop location, all pilgrims traveling to Jerusalem must go up from wherever in Israel they travel. For this reason many call these Psalms the Songs of Ascents.

In Exodus 34:24 God gives Israel a promise contingent upon their observance of these three Pilgrimage Feasts, "*For I will cast out the nations before thee, and enlarge thy borders: neither shall any man desire thy land, when thou shalt go up to appear before the LORD thy God thrice in the year."* Observance of this feast fulfilled one of the conditions of the Mosaic Covenant and assured fellowship with God. Again the idea emerges that, first and foremost, the Feasts of the LORD serve as a spiritual time to honor Israel's covenant-keeping God. The connection to the harvest serves a secondary importance only.

Pentecost paradoxically functions as both a joining link and a separating force between Israel and the Church. Of all the Feasts, this is the only one that both groups observe. Alfred Edersheim points out a unique feature of this feast that symbolizes the linkage: "But what gave to the feast its distinctive peculiarity was the presentation of the two loaves" (262). The modern Christian limits Pentecost to the start of the Church. The modern Jewish person says that Pentecost marks the boundary between the two harvests; a few might also add that Pentecost marks the giving of the Law. Ephesians 2:12-16 reveals the true purpose:

> *That at that time ye were without Christ, being aliens from the commonwealth of Israel, and strangers from the covenants of promise, having no hope, and without God in the world: But now in Christ Jesus ye who sometimes were far off are made nigh by the blood of Christ. For he is our peace, who hath made both one, and hath broken down the middle wall of partition between us; Having abolished in his flesh the enmity, even the law of commandments contained in ordinances; for to make in himself of twain one new man, so making peace; And that he might reconcile both unto God in one body by the cross, having slain the enmity hereby:*

The doctrinal significance of Pentecost lies in the way in which it **joins** the two groups of God's elect. Unless they acknowledge this duality, all studies of Pentecost will end in frustration. As we have already seen, the Feasts serve both a national (Israel) and a universal (all mankind) purpose. Lehman Strauss, referring to Acts 2:1, says that the phrase *"and when the day of Pentecost was fully come"* suggests "the fulfillment of the prophecy in God's prophetic calendar as He gave it in Leviticus 23" (70).

The Doctrinal Meaning

Although most theologians see Pentecost solely as the beginning of the Church, we must never forget that God established the Feasts as a critical part of the Mosaic Covenant, the covenant between Himself and Israel. Any definition of or doctrine derived from Pentecost must therefore **first** consider the nation of Israel's role in the feast. The doctrine pictured by Pentecost, applicable to all Believers, consists of three fundamental elements.

First, Pentecost symbolizes the uniting of Jewish and Gentile believers into one people of God's own choosing. The command of the Pilgrimage Feasts, that all Jewish males must return to Jerusalem, pictures this union. The Pentecost recorded in Acts 2 notes this gathering: "*there were dwelling at Jerusalem Jews, devout men, out of every nation under heaven.*" God started the Church from this "*devout*" group of Jews. As Howard Marshall notes, "Their presence and participation in what happened constituted an indication of the worldwide significance of the event" (70). Notice that the men present were Jewish or Gentile proselytes, not genuine Gentiles. They "acted as a symbol of the universal need of mankind for the gospel and of the church's consequent responsibility for mission" (Marshall 70). This interesting blending of events demonstrates that while God created Pentecost for the Jews, He also used it to mark a significant event in the history of the Church.

Andrew Bonar identifies these two groups of people by periods of time (dispensations). Israel's dispensation, he says, began with the first Passover and ended with the Pentecost of Acts 2. The Church's dispensation began with Pentecost and continues to the present day. "Pentecost may be considered as descriptive of the dispensation that followed, viz. the apostolic Church" (395). His view, however, limits Pentecost to the Church. By so doing, he isolates the Feast of Pentecost from the other six feasts creating an enmity rather than a joining between Jewish and Gentile Believers. Paul, speaking in Romans 1:16, denies this interpretation with its resulting enmity: "*For I am not ashamed of the gospel of Christ: for it is the power of God unto salvation to every one that believeth; to the Jew first and also to the Greek.*"

The harvest that takes place at the time of Pentecost pictures this reconciliation. Like the completed barley harvest, God temporarily completed His dealings with the nation of Israel on the Pentecost of 30 AD. "*I say then, have they stumbled that they should fall? God forbid: but rather through their fall salvation is come unto the Gentiles, for to provoke them to jealousy*" (Romans 11:11). Further, "*that blindness in part is happened to Israel, until the fullness of the Gentiles be come in*" (Romans 11:25). With the completion of the barley harvest, a second harvest, wheat, begins. The wheat harvest symbolizes the Church Age. While Bonar correctly identifies the wheat loaves used at Pentecost as representative of the harvest during the Church Age, he makes the mistake of ruling out Jewish involvement in this dispensation (397). Like many, he sees Pentecost as a distinct line of demarcation, rather than a **shift** in God's dealings with mankind. In this time period, God has shifted His dealings from nations to individuals. It is **not** true to say that God once worked through Jews and now works through the Gentiles. A truer interpretation would say that God worked through a specific nation in the Old Testament and now works through individuals, regardless of their nationality, in the New Testament.

Interestingly, Luke does not use the term "church" (*ekklesia*) in the second chapter of Acts. Alva McClain points out that this omission does not indicate the absence of the Church, but rather it "suggests that it did not yet occupy the center of the stage" (403). In other words, while the Church does occupy a part of God's plan and purpose, it is not the one and only part. A unified interpretation strikes a balance between the ending of the Old Testament nation of Israel, symbolized by the barley harvest, and the beginning of a combined Jewish and Gentile harvest, the Church, symbolized by the wheat harvest. The symbolism of the leaven in the two Pentecost loaves further supports this fusion of Jewish and Gentile believers.

Recall that during the Passover leaven symbolizes permeation, specifically sin's influence and invasion. Israel regarded the Gentiles as the leaven of the world but regarded itself as the holy, pure, and chosen nation. Their viewpoint naturally resulted in friction and enmity between the two groups. Combining this spiritual concept with the physical image of the two crops, one concludes that the two loaves of the feast (Leviticus 23:17) symbolize two prime groups, the Jewish people and the Gentiles. Prior to the Church Age, Gentiles formed the remnant of the total "saved" people. In the Church Age, the Jewish people now become the remnant. Jesus Christ the Messiah, born of a Jewish mother, removes the enmity between the two peoples. Chafer comments that "Jewish and Gentile believers, represented by the two loaves, are united into one body by the baptism of the Holy Spirit" (II:485). Of this feast and this interpretation, Lehman Strauss says,

> The number of the loaves represents the two component parts of the church: believing Jews and believing Gentiles, both having been reconciled to God in one body through faith in the crucified and risen Son of God (Ephesians 2:13-18) (72).

Peter periodically struggled with the idea of Gentiles being included in God's plan for His kingdom (2 Peter 3:15-16). The book of Acts contains much on this subject showing us that many besides Peter struggled with this difficult idea. As both the book of Acts and Church history records, the days of God's working with the nation of Israel had come to an intermission in history. Just as the barley harvest ended at Pentecost and the wheat began, so too, a harvest of national Jewish souls gave way to a predominantly Gentile harvest. The two loaves picture a Church "composed of both Jewish and Gentile believers, purchased by the blood of the Lamb" (Buksbazen 18). Recall also that the sojourner (*ger*) regulations of Pentecost allowed Gentiles to participate in the feast thus foreshadowing the coming "mystery" of the Church. The book of Ruth graphically demonstrates this principle in action.

In the story of Ruth, we see both the Old Testament workings of God as well as a picture of the future. Boaz, a Jewish man, redeems Ruth, a Gentile woman, thus picturing the coming Messiah, Himself a descendant of their union. The Law of Gleanings, described in the book of Ruth, shows that God allows for the stranger and the alien. The provision accorded by the law shows that God still allowed a non-Jewish remnant during the Old Testament period. In the New Testament era, although God has temporarily suspended His dealings with the nation of Israel, He still brings individual Jewish people to Jesus Christ.

The switch of harvest crops on Pentecost reflects the **prime** direction of God's plan and identifies the **prime** group of people. McClain calls this new group, the "royal family in the coming Kingdom" (398). God extends salvation to **all** who come to Him. In the days of Israel's "harvest" (the Old Testament era), a small remnant of Gentiles periodically came to God. On one occasion at least, a larger group came from the city of Nineveh when it repented under Jonah's ministry. So too, during the Gentile "harvest," a remnant of Jewish people will come to Christ (Bonar 400).

Secondly, in the sequence of doctrinal truths, Pentecost symbolizes God's formal offer of the Messiah and the Kingdom. Before He ascended, the Lord had told His apostles and disciples to wait for the coming of the Holy Spirit. During this interval of testing, they were to wait and take no action. Typical of Bible testing, the interval lasted ten days. At the conclusion of this period, fifty days after the Resurrection, on the day of Pentecost, the Holy Spirit descended and gave those gathered the ability to speak in all the languages of the ancient world. When the astonished multitude consisting of Jews and Gentile proselytes, "*devout men, out of every nation under heaven*" (2:5), heard the disciples and followers of Christ speaking in many different languages, they naturally asked, "*What meaneth this?*" (2:12). In response to this, Peter preached a sermon.

The key to his sermon as well as the explanation of the second doctrinal element appears in Peter's opening words: "*Ye men of Judea*" (2:14) and "*Ye men of Israel*" (2: 22). Peter addressed the nation of Israel, not the Church, about the Messiah. In verse 36, he says, "*Therefore, let all the house of Israel know assuredly, that God hath made that same Jesus, whom ye have crucified, both Lord and Christ* [Messiah]." At the Feast of Pentecost, Peter proclaimed Jesus as the long-awaited, promised Messiah. The Messiah's coming fulfilled the promise of the Abrahamic Covenant that stated that Abraham would bring blessings to all the families of earth. A small group "*pricked in their heart*" (2:37) responded resulting in three-thousand newly saved souls.

Unfortunately, three thousand people, large as the sum seems, represented but a small proportion of all those were staying in Jerusalem at the time of this Pilgrimage Feast. Josephus remarks that "a great many ten thousands of men" (468) often came to the Feast of Pentecost, Jewish people from all over the known world (Acts 2:9-11). At the end of Pentecost, the attendees would return to their homes for a period of four months before coming back to Jerusalem for the last cluster of three feasts.

Wherever those present on the Pentecost of Acts 2 went, they spread the news that there were those who claimed that the Messiah had come and had even risen from the dead. Although many did not believe what they had heard, they would still relate the unusual events of this particular Pentecost, the second Pentecost on which God had met with His people as a nation. This appointment held much in common with the historical, first Pentecost.

The events of the Acts 2 Pentecost served not only to honor God but also to offer the Theocratic Kingdom to Israel. Alva McClain believes that the first Pentecost laid the groundwork for this Kingdom (396). On the second Pentecost, God offered Jesus Christ to the Jewish people as their king (402). Out of tens of thousands present, only three thousand responded. As the book of Acts records, God periodically re-offered the Kingdom to Israel. Finally, after many rejections, He postponed the offering and fully opened the Church to the Gentiles. As the number of saved grew (Acts 2:47), the powerful national Jewish leadership felt threatened and reacted with hostility. As the Church became less Jewish in its form of worship, more Gentiles came to Christ.

In Acts 3:19-21 God again formally offered the Theocratic Kingdom to Israel. Had the nation as a whole accepted it, perhaps the fifth appointment would have followed immediately without intermission (McClain 402). Had the nation responded as they had done at Mount Sinai so long ago, Jesus Christ would have returned and started the Theocratic Kingdom. Instead, the nation, led by its high priest, compounded its rejection by killing Stephen (Acts 7) after he had given yet another explanation of God's plan for Israel. From this point on, public miracles in the city of Jerusalem ceased.

As commanded by Christ in Acts 1:8, believers sent the Gospel forth to Judea and Samaria (Acts 8:1-2). The new harvest of sojourners began to come into the storehouse. Like the spreading action of leaven, the Gospel began to spread to the entire world. As more and more believed, however, Israel became more and more hardened. "*What then? Israel hath not obtained that which he seeketh for; but the election hath obtained it, and the rest were blinded* [hardened]" (Romans 11:7). Paul indicates that although God has grafted a wild olive branch into the original plant, He has left an opening for the nation of Israel. Romans 11:23 affirms that "*And they also, if they abide not still in unbelief, shall be grafted in: for God is able to graft them in again.*" Israel's re-grafting must wait, however, for the future, fifth appointment with God when "*the fullness of the Gentiles be come in. And so all Israel shall be saved: as it is written*" (Romans 11:25-26). This future event will bring about the restoration of the Covenant followed by the removal of Israel's national sin, the rejection of the Messiah (Romans 11:27).

Pentecost, therefore, marks the division of the spiritual harvest, necessary because of the national rejection of the Kingdom by Israel. On the first Pentecost at Sinai, some three thousand rejected God's leadership and experienced punishment as a result. On the second Pentecost, three thousand accepted God's plan. The number, unfortunately, fell far short of the entire nation. Paul, speaking of the harvest of Jewish people and Gentiles notes that "*they are not all Israel which are of* [descended from] *Israel*" (Romans 9:6). God's program now harvests those not descended from Israel.

The New Testament often speaks of the harvest. In every passage the context clearly indicates that God refers to a spiritual harvest rather than a physical one. The physical harvest metaphorically portrays God's spiritual work in men. Looking once again at the calendar, one notes that four months of harvest separate Pentecost from the next feast, the Feast of Trumpets. The Lord reminds His disciples of the need to pray regarding the harvest. "*The harvest truly is plenteous, but the laborers are few; pray ye therefore the Lord of the harvest, that he will send forth laborers into his harvest*" (Matthew 9:37-38). Again, in John 4:35, the Lord instructs His disciples, the future founders of the Church, "*Say not ye, There are yet four months, and then cometh harvest? Behold, I say unto you, Lift up your eyes, and look on the fields; for they are white already to harvest.*"

The Pentecost of Acts 2 marked not the end of the relationship between God and Israel but rather the last appointment for many centuries. The four months of harvest symbolize the period of silence between the nation of Israel and its God. While He still speaks to Jewish individuals, God no longer sends prophets to Israel nor does He manifest Himself in the Temple through the Shekinah Glory. In fact, after 70

AD, God removed the Temple itself through the agency of the Romans. Since Israel failed to fulfill its part of the Covenant, God temporarily ended the nation and scattered the Jewish people throughout the world. According to the terms of the Mosaic Covenant, God had to turn from Israel when it rejected Him. He had to curse the land, halt worship, and stop the observance of the Feasts. The unconditional side of the Covenant, however, prevents God from permanently rejecting Israel. Someday, God will end the dispersion and call His people to their next appointment with Him. As a part of its three-part doctrinal function, Pentecost, therefore, secondly symbolizes the national rejection of the Messiah, resulting in God bringing in the "mystery," the Church.

Messiah and the Initiation of the Church

Thirdly, Pentecost symbolizes the start of the worldwide Church, a group of people spiritually separated from the world. Instead of dealing with one nation, God now deals with a united body of nationally diverse people. The Feast of Passover demonstrates God's bringing His chosen people out of Egypt, a picture of the world. The Feast of Unleavened Bread uses the physical nation of Israel to picture the spiritual sanctification of God's people. Historically, the Jewish people demonstrate that God calls His people to be a "*peculiar*" people, set apart to Him. When God temporarily ended the nation of Israel, He allowed the Church to represent Him in the world. In John 15:19 Jesus Christ explains this representation. "*If ye were of the world, the world would love his own; but because ye are not of the world, but I have chosen you out of the world, therefore the world hateth you.*"

The Church, which the Lord builds through the work of the Holy Spirit, now testifies of Him to the world (John 15:26-27). In John 18:36 Christ declares to Pilate that "*My kingdom is not of this world* [age]." Christ's kingdom is the Theocratic Kingdom that will come during His future thousand-year reign (the Millennium) after "*this world.*" In Acts 1:8 the Lord declares that when the Holy Spirit comes (on Pentecost), they "*shall be witnesses unto me both, in Jerusalem, and in all Judea, and in Samaria, and unto the uttermost part of the earth.*" The "*both*" speaks of the Jewish person, represented by Jerusalem and Judea, and the Gentile, represented by Samaria and "*the uttermost part of the earth.*" In 2 Corinthians 6:16 Paul describes the Church as the *"temple of the living God."* God no longer dwells in a physical temple located in Jerusalem; instead, He now dwells in individual hearts, an international temple. Speaking of this change, God reiterates the words given to the nation of Israel at Sinai,

> *I will dwell in them and walk in them; and I will be their God, and they shall be my people. Wherefore come out from among them and be ye separate, saith the Lord, and touch not the unclean thing: and I will receive you, and will be a Father unto you, and ye shall be my sons and daughters. saith the Lord Almighty.*
>
> 2 Corinthians 6:16-18

During the Church Age, God's people still honor Him and give Him glory through their individual, representative lives. They are not a nation, but a people. They claim the New Covenant, not the Abrahamic or Mosaic Covenants. Someday, however, God will end His dealings with the Church and remove it from the world to Himself (1 Thessalonians 4:16-18). He will then graft Israel back into the place reserved for it and He will begin the final harvest pictured by the fruit harvest.

Pentecost, through these three doctrinal elements, draws a line of demarcation in terms of Biblical history. The first four feasts of Israel contain both national (Israel) and universal (mankind) aspects. On the first appointment (Passover), God redeemed a nation. At the second appointment (Unleavened Bread), He sanctified His newly born nation. God showed the first aspect of the Abrahamic Covenant, resurrection, to His people on the third appointment (First Fruits). Lastly, on the fourth appointment, Pentecost, God offered the Promised One to the nation of Israel, an offer which, if accepted, would have brought in the Theocratic Kingdom. These first four appointments establish a clear and significant pattern.

By considering the calendar and the relationship of the seven Feasts to each other, we note that a gap of four months intervenes between Pentecost and the next feast, the Feast of Trumpets. Many hold that these four months represent the period of time between the completed historical events of the first four feasts and the future events yet to come on the last three. In Israel's history, the events of the first four feasts spanned a forty-year period (the Wilderness Period). The same four, over the forty-day period between the Lord's resurrection and ascension, also provided applications for all Believers.

We have shown that significant national events did, in fact, occur on the first four feasts. As we study the last three, however, difficulties arise. The Scriptures fail to mention definite historical events or universal applications connected with the final three feasts (Trumpets, Day of Atonement, and Tabernacles). At this point in history, the last three feasts are incomplete from a historical and a universal standpoint. Both the gap in time and the lack of national significance suggests a future element and application to these remaining feasts. Speaking of this apparent difficulty, Lehman Strauss says,

> Here (Leviticus 23) is an orderly unfolding of the prophetic panorama, reserved in clarity for the student who will take the time to study it carefully. Here the student will see the prophetic and practical import unfold in progressive and harmonious array (8).

In the same vein, Warren Wiersbe asserts that "the general scope of God's prophetic program is given to us in Leviticus 23" (8). Bonar, Wiersbe, Strauss, and McClain all recognize a future fulfillment in the remaining three feasts.

As already stated in Chapter 1, we believe that the positions of the Feasts in the God-appointed calendar show great significance. Just as redemption must come before sanctification and positional sanctification must come before the beginnings of ultimate blessing, so too the fulfillment of the Abrahamic Covenant must come as a prerequisite to future blessing (Pentecost 93). Israel's current rejection causes, not termination, but a delay of God's plans. The three Pilgrimage Feasts naturally suggest that we should divide the Feasts into three groups. Since the first two clusters of feasts clearly apply to Israel and since the Pilgrimage Feasts bring all Jewish men to Jerusalem, we come to the inevitable conclusion that the final cluster of feasts will also apply to the nation of Israel and will center upon Jerusalem.

As we know, the Jewish people can only correctly celebrate the Feasts in Jerusalem. In order for such a future celebration to come about, God must re-gather His people to Jerusalem before the Feasts can resume. We hold, therefore, that the delay between Pentecost and the Feast of Trumpets serves a God-given purpose owing to God's full control over all events. Further, God appears to be using the time gap to develop the "mystery" of the Church and its role in history. We must always remember that the Church never celebrates the Feasts nor did God create the Feasts for the Church. Although the Church recognizes Pentecost, most Believers fail to understand or acknowledge this feast as a primarily Jewish event that also has universal applications for all Believers.

Just as surely as the autumn season comes and brings with it the third group of feasts, so too will God remember His unconditional promise to Abraham and the nation of Israel. The tie between the Abrahamic Covenant and prophecy leads many to seek prophetic fulfillment in the Feasts. Dwight Pentecost says of this relationship,

> . . . this covenant [Abrahamic] has a most important bearing on the doctrines of Eschatology. The eternal aspects of this covenant, which guarantee Israel a permanent national existence, perpetual title to the land of promise, and the certainty of material and spiritual blessing through Christ, and guarantee Gentile nations a share in these blessings, determine the whole eschatological program of the Word of God (71).

Strauss also sees a link between the Covenant and prophecy. "Leviticus 23 projects more prophecy and presents more of God's plan for Israel than any other chapter we can call to mind. Step by step, from commencement to consummation, the divine purpose graphically unfolds" (13).

CHAPTER 7:
THE FEAST OF TRUMPETS

And it shall come to pass in that day, that the great trumpet shall be blown, and they shall come which were ready to perish in the land of Assyria, and the outcasts in the land of Egypt, and shall worship the Lord in the holy mount at Jerusalem.

Isaiah 27:13

The Feast of Trumpets, also known as the Feast of Remembrance or the Feast of Memorial, appears fifth in the sequence of feasts instituted in Leviticus 23. Many view it as a "mystery" feast since the Scriptures never specifically say what this feast memorializes or why trumpets appear as a part of the ritual. Unfortunately, many modern Christian and Jewish writers connect the Feast of Trumpets with the Jewish New Year (*Rosh Hashana*). In reality, Scripture never links the Feast of Trumpets with the New Year in any way. The *true* Jewish New Year (regardless of modern observance) occurs in the First Month of the year, not in the Seventh Month in which the Feast of Trumpets appears. Exodus 12:2 clearly states that the month in which Passover occurs marks the beginning of the Jewish year: "*This month shall be unto you the beginning of months; it shall be the first month of the year to you.*"

Why this change from the spring (the First Month) to the autumn (the Seventh Month)? Scholars suggest a number of reasons. Victor Buksbazen mentions that

> The ancient Rabbis believed that the Lord created the world in the first week of the month of Tishri. Therefore, the first day of the seventh month is considered the beginning of creation and the beginning of the year, hence the present Jewish time reckoning (24).

Others believe that the shift reflects the Jewish civil calendar rather than the sacred one used in the Bible. Edersheim mentions that "Josephus and most Jewish writers maintain, the distinction between the sacred and civil years dates from the time of Moses" (298). Still others think that the Babylonian captivity may have influenced the Jewish people causing them to change their year. Since many ancient cultures placed the New Year in the autumn, this suggestion is logical.

Regardless of the reason, however, the modern Jewish calendar does not coincide with the original Scriptural calendar and should not, therefore, be used in the study of the Feasts. Both the Bible and the Torah use the sacred calendar exclusively. For this reason, and since the Bible is, after all, our sole authority, we must conclude that the modern linkage of *Rosh Hashana* with the Feast of Trumpets is of purely human origin.

In summary, Israel uses a single, unified calendar for its sacred time reckoning. The start of the civil year does begin on the first of Tishri (the Seventh Month), but the start of the sacred year begins on the first of Nisan (the First Month), exactly as Scripture specifies. The *Rosh Hashana* dilemma serves a useful purpose, however. It reminds us, as students of the Scripture, always to handle tradition with care. Although traditions often shed useful light on historical studies, we must never give them precedence over clear Biblical teaching.

The Biblical instructions for the Feast of Trumpets appear in two places: Leviticus 23:23-25 and Numbers 29:1-6. The Numbers passage contains the mechanical details relating to the sacrifices of the feast. Leviticus provides the spiritual teachings:

> *And the Lord spake unto Moses, saying, Speak unto the children of Israel, saying, In the seventh month, in the first day of the month, shall ye have a sabbath, a memorial [remembrance] of blowing of trumpets, a holy convocation. Ye shall do no servile work therein, but ye shall offer an offering made by fire unto the Lord.*
>
> Leviticus 23:23-25

The names by which we know this feast come from verse 24: the Feast of Trumpets, the Feast of Blowing, the Feast of Remembrance, or the Feast of Memorial.

The Feast Is a Memorial

A proper understanding of this feast begins with a study of the word "memorial." In the English language, the word refers primarily to the sense of recalling something, someone, or a particular event. In all cases, the recollection refers solely to the past. A look at the Hebrew root stem (*zikar*), however, reveals far more than the English definition conveys. *Zikar* adds the idea "to remember, recall, call to mind usually as affecting present feelings, thought or action" (*BDB* 269). While this expanded meaning does not change the basic sense of a memorial looking back to the past, it adds the new dimension of the past event affecting present and future actions.

Thomas McComiskey lists three types of remembrances associated with this word. The first type refers to an "inward mental act" that reflects solely on the past event. The second type refers to an "inward mental act" that results in "appropriate external acts." The third type of remembrance refers to "audible speaking" such as recitation. Unfortunately, as McComiskey notes, "it is frequently difficult to decide which of the above meanings best fits a particular passage" (*TWOT* 241).

Leviticus 23:24 poses just such a problem. Scripture does not indicate which past event receives remembrance on the Feast of Trumpets nor does it specify the desired action that should follow this remembrance. Contrast this situation with that described in Exodus 13:8-9 when the

Lord specifically instructs Moses to remind the people of His bringing them out of Egypt. The Lord even provides fathers with an appropriate recitation in answer to their sons' questions about Passover: "*This is done because of that which the LORD did unto me when I came forth out of Egypt*" (Exodus 13:8). In every other passage of Scripture in which the word "memorial" appears, the passage also states the reason for the memorial. The Feast of Trumpets appears to be the one and only exception to this rule. Further, the recitations that accompany other memorials are conspicuously absent. Since these absences seem to exclude the first and third definitions of the word, the only remaining viable definition is the second: "mental acts accompanied by appropriate external acts" (*TWOT* 241).

Scripture supports this conclusion in a number of places. In Exodus 2:24 God remembers His Covenant (looks to the past) and then delivers His people (present action). In Hosea 7:1-2 God remembers His people's sins and responds by withholding His present favors. God healed Hezekiah when He remembered Hezekiah's past faithfulness (2 Kings 20:3). The floodwaters subsided when God remembered Noah (Genesis 8:1). In fact, the Scriptures contain numerous examples of men's present actions occurring as a result of their remembrances. These examples clearly establish precedence in Scripture for McComiskey's second definition of "remembrance."

To Remember . . .	
Recall Only	Inward Mental Act
Recitation	To Verbally Repeat Stored [mentally] Data
Biblical Remembering . . .	To Recall Past Promise or Event To Think on That Promise or Event To Act Outwardly in Response

Figure 11 – Biblical Meaning of Remember

One significant point does emerge when we consider the concept of "remembrance." Although the word remembrance (*zikkaron*) does appear in a number of places in the Scriptures, it occurs primarily in conjunction with one feast, the Feast of Trumpets. We must therefore be especially alert for instances of *zikkaron* when they appear, since they may be clues connected to the Feast of Trumpets.

The real mystery in the Feast of Trumpets lies in the fact that as a memorial it apparently neither reminds one of a past event nor does it seem to promote a resultant action. Memory cannot experience stimulation without a recollection. Since the Scriptures declare the feast a memorial, however, the associated recollection must either come from an event prior to Mount Sinai or from an event yet to come. Thus the feast may hold a prophetic significance.

Tradition offers little reliable help with regards to this feast. At first glance, both the Scriptures and Jewish tradition conspire against us to conceal the true meaning of the feast. Of course, if God has deliberately concealed the meaning of the feast, no amount of study will reveal it. Such a conclusion does not make good sense, however, since the Scriptures fully define the other six feasts instituted in the same passage as the Feast of Trumpets. We must therefore conclude that God may have temporarily masked the meaning of the feast until such a time as He chooses to reveal it. Scripture offers an example of this type of "masking" in the "mystery" of the Church.

> *For I would not, brethren, that ye should be ignorant of this mystery, lest ye should be wise in your own conceits; that blindness in part is happened to Israel, until the fulness of the Gentiles be come in. And so all Israel shall be saved . . .*
>
> Romans 11:25-26

God temporarily masks the meaning of the Church and the role of Jesus Christ to the nation of Israel as a whole. Although individual Jewish people will come to recognize both Jesus Christ and the Church, only the Christians understand the mystery of the Church corporately.

It may also be possible to penetrate this mystery by searching the Scriptures for appointments or great historical events that occur in proximity to this feast. By looking for common patterns among such occurrences, we may be able to deduce both the past event commemorated by the feast as well as the present or future action that occurs as a result of this remembrance. Logic dictates that we look for possible appointments in the history that occurs after Leviticus 23. As it turns out, three such events appear in the Old Testament. Fortunately, these three events also shed enough light to enable us to draw a conclusion about the purpose of the Feast of Trumpets.

The First Historical Event

1 Kings 8 and 2 Chronicles 5 contain parallel accounts of the events surrounding the dedication of the First Temple, built by Solomon in 960 BC. 2 Chronicles 5:3 mentions the time of the dedication: "*Wherefore all the men of Israel assembled themselves unto the king in the feast which was in the seventh month.*" Twenty-three days later the celebrations ended and the people returned to their homes (2 Chronicles 7:10).

Although the Scriptures do not specifically identify the "*feast*" mentioned in this passage, the Hebrew word employed (*hag*) usually refers to the three Pilgrimage Feasts (Passover, Pentecost, and Tabernacles). Recall from Chapter 1 that the Feasts actually fall into three "clusters," each containing a Pilgrimage Feast. The Pilgrimage Feast in each cluster serves to gather the people together who normally remain to observe the other feasts in the cluster as well. *Figure 12* shows the Feasts grouped into clusters.

GROUP NAME	PASSOVER	PENTECOST	TABERNACLES
1st Feast	Passover	Pentecost	Trumpets
2nd Feast	Unleavened Bread	-----------------------	Day of Atonement
3rd Feast	First Fruits	-----------------------	Tabernacles

Figure 12 – Pilgrimage Feasts or *Hag* of Scriptures

Most commentators do not attempt to identify the feast mentioned in 2 Chronicles 5:3. C. F. Keil suggests that the feast may have been the Feast of Tabernacles (III:119). Although this suggestion has merit since the use of *hag* would seem to refer to the Pilgrimage Feast of Tabernacles, another equally reasonable explanation offers another possibility. In the context of the passage, the use of *hag* may actually refer to the entire cluster of feasts (Trumpets, Day of Atonement, and Tabernacles) rather than the single Pilgrimage Feast of Tabernacles that served to gather the people for the occasion. If this interpretation is the true one, then the Temple dedication per... ...ould probably have commenced on the first feast of the triad (the Feast of Trumpets) and continued through the other two.

2 Chronicles 5:12 supports this hypothesis when it mentions that the priests blew trumpets as a part of the dedication: "*and all the Levitical singers . . . with cymbals, harps, and lyres, stood at the east of the altar, and with them a hundred and twenty priests sounding with trumpets.*" Back in Numbers 10:2, God instructed Moses to "*make yourself two trumpets of silver, of hammered work you shall make them; and you shall use them for summoning the congregation . . .*" He further adds in Numbers 10:10

Also in the day of your gladness, and in your solemn days [appointed feasts], *and in the beginnings of your months, ye shall blow with the trumpets over your burnt offerings, and over the sacrifices of your peace offerings; that they may be to you for a memorial* [reminder – zikkaron] *before your God: I am the LORD your God.*

This passage suggests a possible connection between the Feast of Trumpets and the opening events of the dedication. First, the priests blew trumpets. Instead of the traditional two trumpets, however, they blew 120. Solomon may have ordered the extra trumpets in order to make his dedicational blowing even more special than that which occurred on an ordinary Feast of Trumpets observance. Remember also that the word *zikkaron* when used in the context of feasts and the blowing of trumpets appears to refer only to the Feast of Trumpets. If examples of *zikkaron* appear in the passages surrounding Solomon's dedication, they will help to support the idea that the feast in question is, in fact, the Feast of Trumpets.

As it turns out, the passages surrounding the dedication **do** contain several instances of *zikkaron*. In 2 Chronicles 6:42 Solomon prays that the LORD God will "*remember* [zikkaron] *the mercies of David thy servant.*" Immediately after the prayer, God sends fire from heaven to consume the offering and then fills the Temple with His glory. The presence of trumpets and remembrances give strong support to the idea that the dedication began on the Feast of Trumpets.

A close look at the length of the dedication offers one final proof that the feast in question was the Feast of Trumpets. 2 Chronicles 7:10

mentions that the dedication lasted a total of twenty-three days. By adding up the length of all three feasts (Trumpets, Atonement, and Tabernacles) along with the days of the dedication proper, we get exactly twenty-three days. If the feast in question were either the Day of Atonement or the Feast of Tabernacles, the total would fall short of twenty-three. *Figure 13* shows the sequence of the dedication events assuming that the dedication commenced on the Feast of Trumpets.

Seventh Month													
1	2	3	4	5	6	7	8	9	10	11	12	13	14
Feast of Trumpets 1 day	Days of Dedication (Cleansing) 7 days								Day of Atonement 1 day				
15	16	17	18	19	20	21	22	23	24	25	26	27	28
	Feast of Tabernacles 8 days							People went home					

Figure 13 – Proposed Sequence of Events During Temple Dedication

The Significance of the First Event

Having demonstrated the likelihood that the Feast of Trumpets formed a part of the Temple dedication, we must now turn to the important task of collecting the noteworthy events that occurred during the dedication in order to help illuminate the otherwise obscure picture of the Feast of Trumpets. We must begin by reviewing the salient characteristics of the Temple dedication and the history of the Temple itself.

Once Solomon finished the Temple, Jerusalem became the only place where legitimate sacrifices could be offered. Prior to the completion of the Temple, the Jewish people sacrificed in a variety of locations (the Wilderness and Shiloh being two examples). From the beginning of Israel's national history, however, God made it clear that He would choose a **specific** location for all sacrifice. Deuteronomy 12:13-14 explains:

Take heed to thyself that thou offer not thy burnt offerings in every place that thou seest: but in the place which the Lord shall choose in one of thy tribes, there thou shalt offer thy burnt offerings, and there thou shalt do all that I command thee.

At the time when Moses penned this passage, God had not yet specified a location for the future Temple. Years later, David took possession of the Jebusite city of Jerusalem and established it as his national capital. During his reign he committed a serious sin by commissioning a census (2 Samuel 24:10), something that the LORD had specifically forbidden. The LORD offered David three different punishments as a consequence of his sin. David chose the third, a three-day pestilence upon the land.

As the pestilence advanced through the land killing 70,000 men, David begged the LORD for mercy. The LORD stopped the plague's advance at "*the threshing place of Araunah the Jebusite*" on Mount Moriah in Jerusalem and ordered David to "*go up, rear an altar unto the LORD in the threshing floor*" (2 Samuel 24:16, 18). David purchased the threshing floor and performed the required sacrifice. God subsequently decreed that the threshing floor would be the location of the future Temple. Interestingly enough, this same spot before had been the location of Abraham's "sacrifice" of Isaac (Genesis 22:2) many years before.

While David earnestly wished to construct a temple for the LORD, the Scriptures indicate that God commanded otherwise:

And David said to Solomon, My son, as for me, it was in my mind to build a house unto the name of the LORD my God: but the word of the LORD came to me saying, Thou hast shed blood abundantly, and hast made great wars; thou shalt not build a house unto my name, because thou hast shed much blood upon the earth in my sight . . . a son shall be born to thee . . . his name shall be Solomon . . . he shall build a house for my name.

1 Chronicles 22:7-10

Solomon constructed the Temple over a seven-year period using 150,000 workers and the materials accumulated by his father, David. He built the Temple "*at Jerusalem in mount Moriah, where the LORD*" *appeared unto David his* [Solomon's] *father, in the place that David had prepared in the threshing floor of Araunah the Jebusite*" (2 Chronicles 3:1). The dedication took place in the Seventh Month.

By examining the Scriptures that describe the events of the dedication, we find that six happenings emerge as significant:

- **The Ark of the Covenant was placed in the Temple (5:7).**
- **The Shekinah glory came down (7:1).**
- **The Abrahamic and Mosaic Covenants were renewed (6:11).**
- **Sacrifices were started on the designated altar (7:1, 4).**
- **The Feasts were observed covenantally (8:13).**
- **The people gathered as a nation to meet their God and honor Him (6:13).**

It immediately becomes apparent that the events surrounding the dedication of the Temple and, by extension, the Feast of Trumpets focus on the Covenant. The people looked back to the Covenant and renewed their commitment to its conditions. This renewed commitment included the observance of the Feasts as well as sacrifices. God responded immediately and in a visible manner. The conditions of a "memorial" are therefore met: the people looked back and then performed an action as a result of their remembrance. Similarly, God looked back to Covenant and performed an action as a result.

At this point, the information assembled is insufficient for us to draw definite conclusions about the Feast of Trumpets. Since the events of the feast coincided with the Temple dedication, we cannot be sure that the significant happenings pertain solely to the feast itself. Nevertheless, we have advanced forward in our efforts to illuminate this otherwise obscure feast. As we study other instances of this feast, we can compare them to this event. If the significant events again recur, we can begin to draw conclusions about the feast.

The Second Historical Event

The next event to center upon the Feast of Trumpets occurred 400 years after the dedication of the First Temple in 538 BC. In the intervening years, the nation had fallen away from its covenant relationship with God. Idolatry had replaced true worship and the nation lived in spiritual adultery. As a consequence of this national sin, God, acting according to His covenant promises, sent the nation into exile for seventy years. God did not reject His people, however, for in Jeremiah 29:10 He promised "*that after seventy years be accomplished at Babylon I will visit you, and perform my good word toward you, in causing you to return to this place.*"

In fulfillment of the Covenant, God would bring this promise to pass when "*ye* [the people] *call upon me, and ye shall go and pray unto me, and I will hearken unto you and ye shall seek me, and find me when ye shall search for me with all your heart*" (Jeremiah 29:12-13). Ezra 1:1-2 records that God stirred up Cyrus the Persian king to allow a remnant to return to Jerusalem and rebuild the Temple. The remnant, returning in 538 bc, acted as "*one man*" and rebuilt the Temple and the altar (Ezra 3:1). Upon the completion of the restoration work, the people "*from the first day of the seventh month began to offer sacrifices*" (Ezra 3:6). Three familiar patterns appear on this occasion:

- **The people gather as a nation (3:1).**
- **They offer sacrifices in the Temple on Mount Moriah (3:6).**
- **They renew the covenantal observances of the Feasts (3:4-5).**

Obviously, these events bear a close resemblance to some of the events that occurred at the time of the original dedication.

All of these events came about as a result of Ezra and the people's prayers. Ezra "assumed the role of intercessor *and* participant. As he pleaded on behalf of the people, he included himself so that somehow God might see his personal plea as indicative and substitutionary of a national plea" (Rodgers 371). In order to observe the Feasts and perform the sacrifices, the Covenant stipulated that the people must be in the land and gathered at the correct location. The people, therefore, could not observe the Feasts while they were in Babylon.

During the dedication of the First Temple, the glory of God, known as the Shekinah, filled the Temple. Although the Scriptures never specifically use the term "Shekinah," both Jewish people and Gentiles have used the term to describe "the visible divine Presence, especially when resting between the cherubim over the mercy seat" (Unger 1008-

9). Herbert Wolf points out that the Shekinah never filled the Second Temple as it had done in Solomon's day. Instead, the Second Temple waited until the time when Jesus Christ Himself would enter its doors (Luke 2:32) in His incarnate form (37).

Note lastly, that on the occasion of the Second Temple dedication, the people observed all three feasts connected with the Pilgrimage Feast (Tabernacles) just as they probably did at the time of the original dedication. The similarities between the two dedications not only support the notion that the unnamed feast of 2 Chronicles was the Feast of Trumpets but also serve to illuminate further the nature of the Feast of Trumpets.

The Third Historical Event

Wood tells us that the third historical event to fall on the Feast of Trumpets happened in 444 BC (404). Nehemiah 3:26 recounts how the people gathered together near the Temple to hear the first formal sermon recorded in the Bible. "*And Ezra the scribe stood upon a pulpit of wood . . . and Ezra opened the book in the sight of all the people*" (Nehemiah 8:4-5). Remember, the people had only recently come out of Babylon after a long exile. Few probably understood Hebrew and thus did not know the Scriptures. As a result, Ezra had to translate and then explain the Hebrew Scriptures to the crowd of people gathered for the sermon (Nehemiah 8:8).

A great revival followed the message as the Scriptures convicted the people of their national sin. "*For all the people wept, when they heard the words of the law*" (Nehemiah 8:9). As a result of this conviction, the people turned back to the LORD and the Covenant. They began observing the Feasts and purged the nation of sinful practices (Nehemiah 8:14). This national revival took place on "*the first day of the seventh month,*" the Feast of Trumpets (Nehemiah 8:2). Based upon the Biblical record, it becomes clear that the people observed the Feast of Trumpets spontaneously in response to God's providential influence and call (brought about by His remembering them). In summary, on the Feast of Trumpets the following happened:

- **The people gathered as a nation to honor God (8:1).**
- **They sacrificed according to covenant instructions (8:10).**

- **They renewed their covenant relationship with God (9:1-38).**
- **They began to celebrate the Feasts (8:13-18).**

Through a renewed understanding of the Scriptures, the people re-established their Covenant with their God. Nehemiah summed up the results of the revival in his last verse, "*remember me, O my God, for good*" (Nehemiah 13:31). With these words, the historical section of the Old Testament closes.

The Significance of the Three Events

The three historical events that we have examined all share common features. All three occurred on the Feast of Trumpets. We may therefore draw some inferences about the function of this mystery feast. In order to draw these conclusions, we must first look at the events common to each historical observance of the feast:

- **The people gather and act as a nation.**
- **They gather in Jerusalem near the Temple.**
- **They renew their covenant relationship with God.**
- **They begin sacrifices.**
- **They celebrate the Feasts.**
- **God responds to the people on a national level.**

These common elements provide sufficient material to suggest both the "back looking" part of remembrance as well as the "action" that follows the retrospection. In each of the three historical events, the people, acting as a nationally rather than individually, look back to the promises of the Covenant. They see their own failure to follow their part of the Covenant and consequently repent. Their repentance takes the form of a renewed covenant relationship expressed by sacrifices and observance of the Feasts. God, on His part, remembers His role in the Covenant, and acts positively towards His people. It would seem, therefore, that the Feast of Trumpets serves to commemorate the Covenant and the associated benefits that result from being in a covenantal relationship. Furthermore, the feast emphasizes the fact that Jerusalem and the Temple figure closely in this relationship. Finally, the feast serves to stimulate the people to reject sin and to seek their God.

All seven feasts act as indicators of the covenantal state of the nation Israel and its relationship to God. According to the conditions of the Mosaic Covenant, Israel will and must observe the Feasts in its own land. When the nation disobeys the conditions of the Covenant, God exiles it from its land thus preventing it from observing the Feasts. Jerusalem serves as a symbol of the entire land. When God takes Jerusalem from His people, they are not in a right relationship to Him. Daniel portrays this association when he prays towards Jerusalem three times a day (Daniel 6:10). Jerusalem serves as a focal point symbolizing a right covenant relationship between God and His people. Although the Feasts as a whole symbolize the covenant relationship, the Feast of Trumpets seems to emphasize this relationship even more strongly.

The Necessary Future Event

The three events that we have just examined show definite significance and certainly satisfy the memorial aspect of the Feast of Trumpets, but they somehow fall short when compared to the historical events behind the previous four feasts. By reviewing Israel's history, we can see that each of the previous feasts shows a strong correlation with a significant event in Israel's history. Although the Temple dedication, the return from Babylon, and the revival under Nehemiah all have historical significance, none seems as significant as the events leading up to the Passover or the entry into the Promised Land. At first glance, it would seem that the Feast of Trumpets still remains something of a mystery feast. Perhaps, however, the real significance in the Feast of Trumpets does not lie in the past but rather in the future. We must therefore search the Scriptures to see if any event in Israel's future history appears comparable in magnitude to the events associated with the Feasts of Passover, Unleavened Bread, First Fruits, and Pentecost.

Many modern premillennial writers see the Rapture as fulfilling this role (Wiersbe 73). Perhaps the blowing of trumpets on the feast suggests the connection. Unfortunately, this interpretation conflicts with the pattern demonstrated by the Feasts as a whole. Instead, we see the Feast of Trumpets as playing an entirely different role. We will examine the Rapture connection later in this chapter. First, however, we will propose what we see as a much more consistent and much more significant future event.

The Next Event: God's Remembrance

In the book of Lamentations, Jeremiah the prophet laments over the dispersion of Israel in 586 BC. He ends the book with a question of importance to the Jewish nation as well as to God since His faithfulness rests upon the answer: "*Wherefore dost thou forget us for ever, and forsake us so long time?*" (Lamentations 5:20). Jeremiah prays that God would "*Turn thou us unto thee, O LORD, and we shall be turned; renew our days as of old*" (Lamentations 5:21). Here Jeremiah recognizes that God alone can turn the nation back to Him, but in order to turn the nation, God must first remember it. Consequently, Jeremiah asks for God's remembrance.

The Abrahamic Covenant promises an everlasting relationship between God and the Jewish people. As a part of the Mosaic Law (Israel's constitution), God promises to "*remember my covenant with Jacob, and also my covenant with Isaac, and also my covenant with Abraham will I remember; and I will remember the land*" (Leviticus 26:42). God warned Israel that national calamity would follow if it sinned as a nation. His promised response would be twofold: He would disperse the people from the land and then make the land desolate until such a time as He chose to restore it (Leviticus 26:27-28, 33). God would desolate the visible land as a sign of the invisible spiritual desolation of Israel.

The Babylonian captivity (586 BC), coming as a result of many years of spiritual backsliding, marked the beginning of this dispersion and desolation process. Following the seventy-year Babylonian captivity, approximately 50,000 Jewish people returned to Israel, a number far below the total Jewish world population of the time. Even today, despite the valiant efforts of modern Israel, less than half of the world's Jewish population resides in Israel. Furthermore, no spiritual restoration has, as yet, occurred for the people or for the land. Like the creation as a whole, the land suffers from the sins of men. "*For we know that the whole creation groaneth and travaileth in pain together until now*" (Romans 8:22).

God reassures the Jewish people by promising never to "*destroy them utterly, and to break my covenant with them*" (Leviticus 26:44c). As long as the Jewish people remain dispersed throughout the world in a spiritually darkened state, this promise awaits fulfillment. God's trustworthiness and faithfulness demand a remembrance. As the world slowly turns against the nation of Israel and as its people fear for their safety, the Scriptures offer hope and a reminder of God's promise.

> *And if ye go to war in your land against the enemy that oppresseth you, then ye shall blow an alarm with trumpets; and ye shall be remembered before the Lord your God, and ye shall be saved from your enemies.*
>
> Numbers 10:9

A time will come when Israel will be in the land and beset by enemies. God will remember the nation, turn them back to Him, and restore its covenant relationship with Him. As we see throughout the Scriptures, God's pattern of remembering comes during times of trial. He remembered Noah during the judgment of the world, Abraham during the judgment of Sodom, Rachel and Hannah during their trials of barrenness, and His covenant people, Israel, during the judgment upon Egypt. Well could God say,

> *Thou calledst in trouble, and I delivered thee; I answered thee in the secret place of thunder: I proved thee at the waters of Meribah. Selah. Hear, O my people, and I will testify unto thee: O Israel, if thou wilt hearken unto me; There shall no strange god be in thee; neither shalt thou worship any strange god. I am the LORD thy God, which brought thee out of the land of Egypt: open thy mouth wide, and I will fill it.*
>
> Psalm 81:7-10

God longs to bless His nation according to the terms of the Covenant, but Israel seemingly only seeks blessing during times of trial. Psalm 81, traditionally associated with the Feast of Trumpets, speaks of God's delivering His people from Egypt and the later deliverance at Meribah. The Psalmist reminds Israel that when the nation turns back to God, He always restores it. In verse 13 God laments, *"Oh that my people had hearkened unto me and Israel had walked in my ways."* This passage reflects the desire of a loving God, not One Who has abandoned His people forever.

Scripture indicates that God has judicially blinded national Israel during the present period of history (the Church Age). In 2 Corinthians 3:14-15 Paul explains that their current blindness is only temporary: "*For I would not, brethren, that ye should be ignorant of this mystery, lest ye should be wise in your own conceits; that blindness in part is happened to Israel, until the fulness of the Gentiles be come in.*" Two important facts emerge from this passage. First, God has blinded Israel only "*in part.*" Although the nation as a whole rejects Jesus Christ as Messiah, individual Jewish people will continue to come to recognize Him throughout the Church Age. Second, this blindness will continue only until history reaches the "*fulness of the Gentiles.*" In other words, at the conclusion of the Church Age, God will once again focus on His chosen people, Israel.

God will effect His change of focus at a definite, appointed time. His "remembering" depends upon His redemption plan, for He does not actually forget. Moses (Deuteronomy 28:63-68), Jeremiah (Jeremiah 23:5-8), and Ezekiel (Ezekiel 37) all agree that the "re-gathering" of the people of Israel will foreshadow the coming salvation and kingdom.

> *That then the Lord thy God will turn* [literally end] *thy captivity, and have compassion upon thee, and will return and gather thee from all the nations, whither the Lord thy God hath scattered thee. . . . And the Lord thy God will bring thee into the land.*
>
> Deuteronomy 30:3-5

A careful reading of this passage indicates that spiritual re-establishment of the covenant relationship will come first before the "official" return to the land. The "unofficial" return to the land began in the middle of the Twentieth Century and continues to this day. God says that "*when all these thing are come upon thee*" (Deuteronomy 30:1), meaning after the universal dispersion and desolation of the land, then they shall "*return unto the Lord*" (30:2). The context here indicates a spiritual return, not a physical one since the passage says "*unto the Lord*" and not "unto the land." Note well that this passage *cannot* refer to the postexilic return from Babylon since it specifically says that they would come from "*all the nations*" (30:1) and not just from Babylon.

Maimonides, a great Jewish commentator, taught that the Feast of Trumpets serves as an annual awakening of the people to repentance in preparation for the Day of Atonement (Donin 246). These annual "awakenings" prefigure the greatest re-awakening in history, the day that God in His remembrance will re-gather Israel. God likens Israel's future triumph to the process to a birth. He asks,

> *Who hath heard such a thing? Who hath seen such things? Shall the earth be made to bring forth in one day? or shall a nation be born at once? for as soon as Zion travailed, she brought forth her children. Shall I bring to the birth, and not enable to bring forth? saith the LORD, shall I cause to bring forth, and shut the womb? saith thy God. Rejoice ye with Jerusalem, and be glad with her.*
>
> Isaiah 66:8-10

God will complete the birth process that he started in Egypt on Passover. He used three previous historical observances of the Feast of Trumpets to prefigure the final return to covenant fellowship. The final revival, beginning during a time of great trial for Israel and judgment for the world, will culminate in ultimate restoration for the nation.

> *And it shall come to pass in that day, that the great trumpet shall be blown, and they shall come which were ready to perish in the land of Assyria, and the outcasts in the land of Egypt, and shall worship the Lord in the holy mount at Jerusalem.*
>
> Isaiah 27:13

The great Feast of Trumpets will occur when God "remembers" Israel and begins its revival and re-gathering. At God's appointed time, He will stir the hearts of the Jewish people that are dwelling in the land and in the city of Jerusalem. They will hear His Word, erect an altar, re-institute sacrifices, and observe God's law according to the Covenant. Obviously, this sequence of events requires Israel's national presence in the land, occupation of the city of Jerusalem, and access to the Temple Mount. The Feast of Trumpets, better called the Feast of Remembrance, will follow the pattern that God established through the earlier observances of the Feast of Trumpets. These events will, incidentally, also mark the beginning of the Tribulation period of history. Seen in the light of both past and future events, the Feast of Trumpets does indeed correspond to several significant events in the national history of Israel.

Of course, not all Jewish people will experience an inward heart revival on that day. Individuals then, as now, must still individually recognize Jesus Christ as Lord and Savior. On this occasion, however, Israel will experience revival on a **national** level that will prepare the nation for the cleansing of its national sins. As the Psalmist says in Psalm 22:27, *"All the ends of the world shall remember and turn unto the LORD: and all the kindreds of the nations shall worship before thee."* Here, God speaks of a worldwide turning, where all men will worship the true and living God. Such a situation seems very hard to believe as we look at the world around us. Man in his depravity will certainly not turn to God of his own accord. It will take a miracle, one made possible only by God Himself.

Why the Feast of Trumpets Is Not the Rapture

As we have already mentioned, many believe that the Feast of Trumpets marks the time of the Rapture of the Church. The blowing of trumpets on both occasions probably suggests the idea. Unfortunately, this assumption runs contrary to a number of evidences and patterns demonstrated by the Scriptures. First and foremost, Rapture is an event for the **Church** not one for the nation of Israel. Although the Feasts do offer universal doctrinal teachings for the Church, they exist primarily for the nation of Israel. Many writers work around this objection by making the re-awakening of Israel simultaneous with the Rapture (Wiersbe 12). While such a confluence of events could be the case, this view still dilutes the significance of the Feast of Trumpets and diverts its focus from its primary recipient, Israel.

In all likelihood, a small interval of time (less than one year) will divide the Rapture from the start of the Tribulation (and it's accompanying national re-awakening of the Jewish people). This assumption is logical for two reasons. First, in Matthew 24:36 Christ specifically indicates that, other than the Father, no one knows when the Rapture will happen. If the Rapture were to occur on the Feast of Trumpets, Christians around the world would have the means of predicting the Rapture. They could then annually await Christ's collection of the Church every September. Such a notion runs contrary to the doctrine of immanency (the concept that Christ can return at any moment), something that John 14:2-3, 1 Corinthians 15:51-52, and Revelation 22:20 all support.

Second, if Rapture were to occur simultaneously with the start of the Tribulation, the re-awakening of Israel would be mixed with the removal of the Church. Such a blending of two significant events would probably cause a great deal of confusion, something abhorrent to God. In all likelihood, God will separate the two events by a small interval of time so that the recently re-awakened Jewish people will fully understand their role in God's plan without the added confusion a simultaneous Rapture.

Once God removes the veil from Israel's collective eyes, it will turn back to the LORD and recognize Jesus Christ as their true Messiah. A total of 144,000 Jewish people will be saved and act as evangelists to their fellow Jews and to the world at large (Revelation 7:1-8). This rapid sequence of events will mark what may be termed a "re-awakening" of the nation of Israel. This term should be distinguished from "re-gathering," a term that refers to the collective return of the dispersed Jewish people to Israel. A preliminary re-gathering is happening at this very moment as Jewish people from all over the world return to Israel. During the Tribulation period, the process will probably accelerate as a result of persecutions (Zechariah 12:3) and the overall spiritual re-awakening radiating out from Israel. The final re-gathering, however, will not happen until the conclusion of the Tribulation when all saved Jewish people will come together in Israel under the Lord Jesus Christ's Millennial rule.

The Prophetic Sequence

Since the events described in the previous pages may still seem somewhat convoluted (as prophetic events unfortunately often are), we have compiled the following sequence of events to depict our interpretation of the major events of the End Times. As any student of eschatology will see, this sequence presupposes a pre-Tribulation Rapture view as well as a Premillennial perspective.

- **Israel begins to re-gather in Israel (currently in progress).**
- **World opinion turns against Israel (currently in progress).**

- The Rapture removes the Church (unknown time).
- Unknown interval of time passes (less than one year).
- The Feast of Trumpets
- Israel re-awakens spiritually as a *nation*.
- Two witnesses begin ministry
- 144,000 Jewish people are saved.
- Sacrifices are re-instituted.
- The Covenant is renewed.
- The Feasts are observed.
- The Tribulation begins.
- An accelerated return of dispersed Jewish people to Israel begins.
- Two witnesses die and are resurrected before the world's eyes
- Midway through the Tribulation (3 ½ years later)
- The Antichrist desecrates the Temple.
- The Day of Atonement (7 years later)
- The Tribulation ends.
- Christ Returns (the Second Advent).
- The unrighteous are condemned and removed.
- The saved Jewish people gather to Israel.
- Feast of Tabernacles
- The Millennial reign of Christ begins.
- Great Jubilee
- The New Heavens and New Earth are created.
- The Mystery Solved

Although the Feast of Trumpets continues to remain something of a mystery feast, the preceding explanations and analysis remove a great deal of the mystery and obscurity. Like the preceding four feasts, the Feast of Trumpets will mark yet another "mountain top" experience in the nation of Israel's history. The start of the Tribulation, the nation's national reawakening, the re-institution of the Covenant, and the renewal of sacrifices all fulfill the requirements set by the previous feasts for an event of great national significance. Most importantly, the Feast of Trumpets, also known as the Feast of Remembrance, powerfully demonstrates God's great remembrance and faithfulness to His special covenant people, the nation of Israel.

CHAPTER 8:
THE DAY OF ATONEMENT

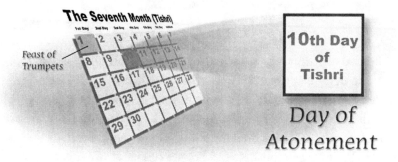

It shall be unto you a Sabbath of rest, and ye shall afflict your souls;

Leviticus 23:32

Our righteous Messiah has departed from us, we are horror stricken, and have none to justify us. Our iniquities and the yoke of our transgressions he carries who is wounded because of our transgression. He bears on his shoulder the burden of our sins, to find pardon for all our iniquities. By his stripes we shall be healed - O Eternal one, it is time that Thou shouldest create him anew!

This ancient Musaf prayer (Buksbazen 43) reflects the plaintive cry of the Day of Atonement, a cry of fear and of awe. The Scriptures give foundation for such a cry in connection with the sixth Feast of the LORD.

And the LORD spake unto Moses, saying, Also on the tenth day of this seventh month there shall be a day of atonement: it shall be an holy convocation unto you; and ye shall afflict your souls, and offer an offering made by fire unto the LORD. *And ye shall do no work in that same day: for it is a day of atonement, to make an atonement for you before the* LORD *your God. For whatsoever soul it be that shall not be afflicted in that same day, he shall be cut off from among his people. And whatsoever soul it be that doeth any work in that same day, the same soul will I destroy from among his people. Ye shall do no manner of work: it shall be a statute for ever throughout your generations in all your dwellings. It shall be unto you a sabbath of rest, and ye shall afflict your souls: in the ninth day of the month at even, from even unto even, shall ye celebrate your sabbath.*

Leviticus 23:26-32

Several aspects set this feast apart from the other six. Only the Day of Atonement begins at sunset, requires a great fast, and specifies a **unique** Sabbath rest period (although other feasts include Sabbaths, the Sabbath of the Day of Atonement is somewhat different). Additionally, its name, "atonement," suggests unique theological overtones to this event. Further, Scripture establishes no link between this feast and a historical or agricultural event. Finally, the Scriptures provide more detailed instructions (in Leviticus 16) for the Day of Atonement than for any other feast. These differences bring us to the inevitable conclusion that God has set this feast uniquely apart. R. K. Harrison calls this uniqueness the "ceremonial and theological pivot" of the entire book of Leviticus (166).

The Unique Aspects of the Day of Atonement

Its starting time sets the Day of Atonement apart from the other Feasts. Scripture instructs the people to begin the feast at sunset the day before the official feast day: "*in the ninth day of the month at even*" (Leviticus 23:32). Although families begin the Passover celebration at evening as well, the Day of Atonement is different in that the **national** celebration begins at sunset.

The word, "*even*," refers to the time of day coming at the very end of daylight hours, the period of twilight, which by Jewish law still qualifies as day (Donin 247). The Hebrew "day" begins when the sun dips below the horizon creating darkness, for the Hebrew day begins with darkness. The Hebrews derive this concept from Genesis 1:1-

2: "*In the beginning . . . and darkness was upon the face of the deep.*"
Darkness seems fitting since this feast generates little joy and happiness
from its celebration. The feast's observance begins covered over with
the solemnity of darkness.

As the light diminishes on the ninth day of the Seventh Month, the
solemnity of the feast engulfs the Jewish person as he, with all Israel,
begins a total fast, acknowledging God's instruction to "*afflict your souls*"
(Leviticus 23:32). During this time he abstains from food and drink
for almost twenty-five hours. The intensity of the fasting emphasizes
the necessary "concentration on the serious business of the nation's sin"
(Morris 69, 80). The mention of afflicting "*souls*" elevates this fast to a
spiritual level and emphasizes national and individual sin.

Israel's neglect of the Sabbath of the land, one of its greatest national
sins, resulted in the seventy-year Babylonian Captivity. The Scriptures
warned Israel of the dire consequences that would follow if the land
did not receive its "*sabbath of rest*" (Leviticus 26:24-25). The passages
pertaining to the Day of Atonement similarly mention a "*sabbath of rest.*"
In each case the phrase employed is a rarely used word combination,
shabat shabbathon. This repetitive expression, which means "sabbath
sabbath" (Leviticus 23:32), reflects the Hebrew grammatical intensive.
Our English translation misses the strength and significance of this
intensive by using two different words instead of repeating the single
word, "sabbath" (Lange 171). This particular intensive combination
appears only in Exodus and Leviticus in connection with three
significant events: the weekly Sabbath, the Day of Atonement, and the
seventh-year land Sabbath (Exodus 31:15, 35:2; Leviticus 16:31, 23:3,
23:32, 25:4). A proper understanding of the uniqueness of the Day of
Atonement requires an understanding of the term "Sabbath" and of its
intensified form that our English Bible translates "*sabbath of rest.*"

Sabbath Sabbath shabat shabbathon	
The Weekly Sabbath	Exodus 31:15, 35:2, Leviticus 23:3
Day of Atonement	Leviticus 16:31, 23:32
Seventh-year land Sabbath	Leviticus 25:4

Figure 14 – Shabat Shabbathon: The Sabbath of Sabbaths

The term, Sabbath conveys serious overtones to the nation of Israel as well as to the individual Hebrew. The root of Sabbath, *shabat*, means "to sever, end or complete" (*TWOT* 903). Thus, the seventh day of the week "completes" or "ends" the week as individuals cease or desist from their normal weekly endeavors. The seventh-year land Sabbath "completes" or "ends" the production of the land, giving it rest for one year.

God gave the Sabbath as a sign to Israel (Exodus 31:17). "*It is a sign between me and the children of Israel for ever: for in six days the Lord made heaven and earth, and on the seventh day he rested and was refreshed.*" Literally, the Sabbath, acting as a sign-post, communicates messages from God to Israel. God first used the Sabbath in this way in Genesis 2:2. He continued the application in Leviticus 23:3 (as we will explore in a later chapter). The use of the Sabbath points Israel to a time of ceasing from its labors with a resultant rest guaranteed by the Covenant. The intensive use of the term in the Day of Atonement further emphasizes a necessary element of that rest: complete atonement. "Thus, the rest in atonement is equal to the rest that was enjoyed in an unfallen creation" (Bonar 387). Man could enjoy fellowship with the Creator only if atonement could wipe away the uncleanness of sin that separates man from a pure and holy God (Keil 445).

Considering this unique use of the term "sabbath sabbath," we conclude that the Day of Atonement must also represent an ending or completion of the atoning work that only God can accomplish. This completion, of course, includes the nation of Israel. To understand the concept fully, however, we must examine the meaning of the name of the feast itself, the Day of Atonement or Yom Kippur (literally *Yom Kippurim*).

Unlike the other feasts which it names with descriptive terms, Scripture names the sixth feast, the Day of Atonement (Leviticus 23:27), with a theological term. The Hebrew root word for atonement, *kaphar*, means "to make atonement or reconciliation" (*TWOT* 452) or "to pacify, make propitiation" (*BDB* 497). The English name, Day of Atonement, comes from the Hebrew *yom kippurim*, a plural noun. Interestingly, both Jewish and Gentile translators render it as a singular noun in English translations. Literally, *yom kippurim* means

"Day of Atonement**s**." Some commentators explain the discrepancy by suggesting that the translators chose the singular word form to emphasize the unity of the day. However, translating the word in this way emphasizes the wrong aspect of the term. The text stresses the objects that receive atonement rather than the day itself.

> *And he shall make an atonement for the holy sanctuary, and he shall make an atonement for the tabernacle of the congregation, and for the altar, and he shall make an atonement for the priests, and for all the people of the congregation.*
>
> Leviticus 16:33

The scriptural instructions clearly apply atonement to five separate categories that include both animate and inanimate items. Many people define atonement as the "covering of sins." Such an explanation seems weak, however, since inanimate objects like the altar do not need "covering" for their "sins" (Bonar note 23). Unfortunately, most Bible students examine atonement from a purely human perspective and tend to ignore the inanimate aspect of the atonement process. Similarly, most theological books focus on the atonement process from the sinner's viewpoint. While such an emphasis is not wrong, it does not encompass fully the Biblical meaning of atonement. Yet the Scripture stresses the term "Day of Atonement**s**" and includes inanimate objects in atonement. A complete definition of atonement must therefore encompass inanimate objects in order to demonstrate how Christ can make atonement for a nation as well as the individuals that constitute that nation. Such a definition will explain the atonement of the Holy of Holies, the altar, and the entire Tabernacle as well as the people in connection with the Day of Atonement. It also shows that atonement does not "cover over" sins but actually **cleanses** them. **When one studies the Scriptures, he must always be careful to follow the teaching of the Scriptures rather than the thinking and traditions of men.**

The All-Encompassing Atonement

Lastly, in order to be truly complete, a proper definition of atonement must include the idea of cleansing. Lehman Strauss points out that "before the nation [Israel] can enjoy lasting peace and protection, repentance and cleansing from sin are imperative" (96). Warren Wiersbe defines three events pictured by the Day of Atonement: "the work of Jesus Christ, the future cleansing of Israel and the future cleansing of the Church" (81). Each of these events expresses the need for removing the contamination of sin from individuals, nations, and objects in God's service, not just a covering over. Leviticus 16, the "theological pivot" of the book, speaks extensively of this need. "Now the focus is upon the making of atonement for all the uncleannesses and sins of inadvertence of the entire Israelite congregation, beginning with the priesthood" (Harrison 167). Samuel Schultz says, "uncleanness was removed from the worshipers [on this feast] and the Tabernacle so that God could be worshipped in purity and holiness" (85).

Both commentators and the Scriptures inescapably link the Day of Atonement to the cleansing of sin. Leviticus 10 indicates that the implements of worship must also be clean. The same chapter describes Nadab and Abihu's sin at the altar of the LORD before the Tabernacle. Their actions and the LORD's subsequent response prompted Moses to instruct Aaron and his other sons in the doctrine of cleansing. This understanding was necessary so:

> *that ye may put difference between holy and unholy, and between unclean and clean; and that ye may teach the children of Israel all the statutes which the LORD hath spoken unto them by the hand of Moses.*
>
> Leviticus 10:10-11

Moses then instructed Israel concerning the cleanness and uncleanness of animals, women, leprosy victims, and issues of the flesh (Leviticus 10 through 15). All of these rituals and commandments serve a single purpose:

> *Thus shall ye separate the children of Israel from their uncleanness; that they die not in their uncleanness, when they defile my tabernacle that is among them.*
>
> Leviticus 15:31

The six chapters between the sin of Aaron's sons and the instructions for the Day of Atonement (Leviticus 16) contextually link the theological cleanliness of Israel to individual *and* national sin. The LORD therefore says, "*I will be sanctified in them* [treated as holy -qadash] *that come near me, and before all the people I will be glorified* [honored]" (Leviticus 10:3). He indicates that His holiness or cleanness must not be diminished by the unclean coming near or touching Him. The word *Qadash* conveys the idea of an object or person being "without evil" (*TWOT* 786). From this definition, we can derive the truth that sinful men can offend the holiness of God through their taint of sin. Leviticus 16 details the proper method of restoring the tainted (sinful) object to a state of holiness or theological cleanness. God establishes sacrificial blood as the only agent suitable for this cleansing process.

A full definition of atonement must also include the process of making an unclean person or object clean (*qadash*). Without such a cleansing process, God can never use a tainted person or object. God demonstrated this cleansing process when He met with Moses on Mount Sinai. Since God's presence, made the mountain *qadash*, Moses had to recognize it as holy ground (Exodus 3:5) before he approached God. This incident helped Moses understand the holiness of the God of Israel. He needed to know the purity of the One Whom he represented before Pharaoh when he acted as God's instrument of deliverance.

Isaiah understood this principle of spiritual cleanliness when upon seeing God face-to-face he realized his own sinfulness and cried, "*Woe is me! For I am undone; because I am a man of unclean lips and I dwell in the midst of a people of unclean lips*" (Isaiah 6:5). This passage reveals that sin is more than just past acts. Instead, sin is an ongoing disqualification, in other words, uncleanness. Isaiah perceived the gulf between the clean God and unclean man. He knew that his uncleanness doomed him in God's presence. The application of a live coal took his "*iniquity . . . away and . . . cleansed*" his sin (Isaiah 6:7). God's action demonstrates that He can make the unclean clean. Once clean, God could send His servant, Isaiah, to deliver a message of condemnation to Israel. These two examples illustrate man's need for spiritual cleansing in order for God to be able to use them in His service.

The Day of Atonement performed this function for the entire nation of Israel. Once each year, on the tenth day of the Seventh

Month, the High Priest entered the Holy of Holies in order to "*make an atonement for you, to cleanse [taher] you, that ye may be clean from all your sins before the LORD*" (Leviticus 16:30). Although the yearly feast temporarily handled the sins of ignorance (Hebrews 9:7), it would take a future atonement using the blood of Christ to deal permanently with sin (Hebrews 9). *Taher* "most frequently [is] used of the purification necessary to restore someone who has contracted impurity to a state of purity so that he could participate in the ritual activities (Lev 22:4-7)." The root of *taher* emphasizes the idea of purity since it refers to the purity of gems. Regarding priests, it indicates that they must be "cleansed to fulfill their ritual functions" (*TWOT* 343).

King David also recognized his need of personal cleansing (Psalm 51:9) before God could bless the nation (Psalm 51:18). Not only kings and priests, but also all of God's people need his cleansing. In Job 4:17 Eliphaz mentions that men need cleansing in order to be righteous with their God. Jeremiah rhetorically asks if Jerusalem can "*be made clean*" (Jeremiah 13:27). He recognized that only God could spiritually cleanse the city of its sin. God, speaking of the future and final restoration of the nation of Israel, declares:

Then will I sprinkle clean water upon you, and ye shall be clean: from all your filthiness, and from all your idols, will I cleanse you. A new heart also will I give you, and a new spirit will I put within you: and I will take away the stony heart out of your flesh, and I will give you a heart of flesh. And I will put my spirit within you and cause you to walk in my statures, and ye shall keep my judgments, and do them. And ye shall dwell in the land that I gave to your fathers; and ye shall be my people, and I will be your God. I will also save you from all your uncleanness . . . In the day that I shall have cleansed you from all your iniquities . . . and they shall know that I am the LORD.

Ezekiel 36:25-38

Only God can *taher* individuals (Psalm 51:9) or nations (Ezekiel 36). Keil associates such a cleansing to "the festival of atonement, which provided for the congregation of Israel the highest and most comprehensive expiation that was possible under the Old Testament"

(I:395). Any definition of atonement that ignores spiritual cleansing and neglects the scriptural declarations of Leviticus 16, 23 and Hebrews 9:22 is incomplete. True cleansing became possible at the Cross which completed the picture of the Day of Atonement. The atonement Christ performed on the Cross applies only to individuals at this time, not to nations or the creation. Someday, however, the atonement will act globally over all creation and over nations. This final form of the atonement will come at the End Times (Hebrews 9:26).

The Act of Atonement: The Cross

The Lord Jesus Christ's death upon the Cross accomplished atonement for individuals through the shedding of His blood. On a future Day of Atonement, He will apply the atonement to the nations as well as to the creation. The entry of sin at the Garden of Eden necessitates such an atonement and cleansing because sin taints and destroys the holiness or *qadash* of people and things. Until Adam sinned, everything in the world was holy and free from the pollution of sin. Sin and its taint followed Adam and Eve out of the Garden and into the creation.

The need for atonement came as a result of that original act of sin. Scholars view sin in a number of ways. Chafer defines it as a "lack of conformity to the character of God" (Walvoord I:367). Another defines four of the Hebrew words for sin as:

- **missing the mark or deviating from the goal (Judges 20:16)**
- **rebellion against God, the defiance of His holy lordship and rule (Isaiah 24:1)**
- **deliberate wrongdoing**
- **straying away from the correct path (Ezekiel 34:6)** (New Bible Dictionary 1116)

Merrill Unger says that sin is "everything in the disposition and purpose and conduct of God's moral creatures that is contrary to the expressed will of God (Romans 3:20; 4:15; 7:7; James 4:12, 17)" (1028). Each definition contributes to an overall picture of sin, but, interestingly, none points out the contamination that results in all those who encounter it. Only God remains free from sin. "*Who shall not fear thee, O Lord, and glorify thy name? For thou only art holy*" (Revelation 15:4).

Thus, God stands in marked contrast to His creation. Since the manifestation of sin diminishes the testimony of God in the world, however, the pure and holy God must separate Himself from mankind. In order to manifest Himself properly in the creation, God must first remove all sin. Atonement purifies everything, both animate and inanimate objects, for God would not be just in requiring His people to be holy "*for I am holy*" (Leviticus 11:44 and 1 Peter 1:16), if He had not provided the means for them to meet His requirements. Redemption, propitiation, and reconciliation provide just such a means.

In order to understand fully the magnitude of God's atonement, we must first understand the gulf that lies between God's holiness and man's sinfulness. As a consequence of their single sin, God banished our first parents from Eden.

> For one sin all of the posterity of the Garden fell under a curse that remains upon them to this day. For one sin God excluded Moses from the Promised Land. For David's one sin, 70,000 men died. For one sin God struck Elisha's servant with leprosy. For one sin God ended the lives of Ananias and Sapphira (Pink 40).

God reveals the seriousness of sin by His righteous response to it. Leon Morris says,

> . . . the concept of the wrath of God stresses the seriousness of sin. On the Old Testament view sin is not just a mere peccadillo which a kindly, benevolent God will regard as of no great consequence. On the contrary, the God of the Old Testament is One who loves righteousness (Psalms 33:5; 48:10; etc.), and whose attitude to unrighteousness can be described as hatred. (174-175)

Atonement removes sin by a process of three steps, the first of which is redemption. Redemption addresses the price of sin, the penalty of sin, and the condemnation of sin that results in both temporal and eternal separation from the holy God (John 3:16-18). Redemption requires a ransom that "involves the payment of a price so that another who is held in bondage may be set free" (McClain and Smith 54). Lewis Chafer adds that Christ "paid in full the price of releasing the sinner from the bondage and judgment of his sins" (Walvoord II:61). Biblically, the ransom for redemption, *kopher*, "refers to the sum paid to redeem a forfeited life" (Morris 24). Such redemption includes both property and things dedicated to the Lord.

The story of Ruth illustrates redemption through the means of a kinsman-redeemer, Boaz (Ruth 4). God beautifully pictured the act of redemption in the Feast of Passover. The Hebrew slaves could never pay the enormous price of redemption from their Egyptian masters, so God had to intervene as their redeemer. So too, with spiritual slavery, a man can never pay the price of his sin. True redemption, therefore, requires the intervention of a Third Party, One capable of paying the enormous price for all mankind (Morris 61).

Christ paid the price of sin to God the Father, not Satan, in order to restore separated man to God. Remember, human sin offended **God,** not Satan. God's righteous justice demanded full payment and redemption. Sin never harmed Satan nor injured his "glory"; man owed Satan nothing. Redemption "offers the sinner release from sin and from the situation of being a bondservant to sin. Redemption results in liberation because the price has been paid to free the sinner from his sin" (Walvoord II:61).

Propitiation or satisfaction marks the second step of atonement. The sacrificial death of Christ upon the Cross **satisfied** God the Father. The Lord Jesus Christ "*is the propitiation* [atonement] *for our sins: and not for ours only, but also for the sins of the whole world*" (1 John 2:2). Christ's death *appeased* [the LXX translation of *kaphar* (McClain and Smith 56)] God's righteous wrath and opened the way for man to be clean and useful to God. God's need to be appeased does not stem from maliciousness; His true justice requires satisfaction through the just and righteous punishment of sin. Atonement through the blood of Christ's sacrifice satisfies God's justice.

The first aspect of atonement pays the ransom price, the second aspect satisfies God's justice, and the third aspect reconciles man to

God. Reconciliation always occurs with respect to two parties, the offender and the offended. According to the Bible, God (the offended) is never reconciled to man (the offender). Rather, man is always reconciled to God. Since man lacks the means to effect reconciliation, God Himself initiated the process of man's reconciliation. That God must initiate the process is quite logical for "if man has come under condemnation so that the sentence of God is against him, then more is required than repentance if man's rightful relationship to God is to be restored" (Morris 245). God therefore sent Jesus Christ to bring about reconciliation through atonement, which then permits God's blessing upon man or, in the case of Israel, upon a nation (2 Corinthians 5:17-21). As used in the New Testament, reconciliation speaks of a complete change (Morris 245). Reconciliation is the "manward aspect of Christ's work on the cross" (Walvoord II:62). Reconciliation removes the condemnation that has fallen upon man through his sin.

A better translation for the Old Testament word "reconciliation" is "making an atonement for sin" (Leviticus 6:30; 8:15; 16:20; 1 Samuel 29:4; 2 Chronicles 29:24; Ezekiel 45:15, 17, 20; Daniel 9:24) (Walvoord II:63). Reconciliation changes both man and the world into a new creation (2 Corinthians 5:19-20, Colossians 1:20). While these passages deal with individuals and their personal salvation, they remind us that the coming reconciliation for the nation of Israel will result in a changed nation. The path to reconciliation is complete, but the process of reconciliation continues as God offers salvation to all people and some receive it: "*Now then we are ambassadors for Christ, as though God did beseech you by us: we pray you in Christ's stead, be ye reconciled to God*" (2 Corinthians 5:20). The door still stands open. Colossians 1:20 further reminds us that reconciliation will be all-encompassing one day, for God will reconcile "*all things unto himself; by him, I say, whether they be things in earth, or things in heaven.*"

Atonement removes the source of pollution (sin's domination in the old nature). The removal of the source leaves only the need for cleansing in order to make that person or object useful to the holy God. Atonement also effects an ongoing change in the individual Christian. John writes that

If we confess our sins, he is faithful and just to forgive us our sins, and to cleanse us from all unrighteousness. . . . And he is the propitiation for our sins: and not for ours only, but also for the sins of the whole world.

1 John 1:8-10

Lewis Chafer points out that

> ...this passage, addressed to Christians, sets forth the fact that no one is without a sin nature nor is anyone without acts of sin. When acts of sin become known to a believer, he is called on to confess this to God immediately. He is then promised continued fellowship with Christ and cleansing by His blood. (Walvoord II:69)

Thus, the cleansing power of atonement prevents further contamination from sin if we confess our sins.

Remembering that atonement applies to inanimate objects as well as to humans, we must also remember that God will atone for Israel as a nation (Ezekiel 36:25-38).

> At the time of Christ's second coming when righteous Israel will be regathered and brought into the land (Jer. 23:5-8), the sins of the godly remnant will be forgiven, and they will then experience the grace of God in the millennial kingdom. . . . The death of Christ makes it possible for God . . . to restore and bless the nation Israel in fulfillment of her covenants. (Walvoord II:72, 73)

Clearly, national Israel needs reconciliation to its God. The Scriptures speak of a coming day when the nation will once again worship God, the time when He will graft it back into the vine (Romans 11:25-27). At that time He will *"take away their sins."* The fact that Paul mentions this event as taking place in the future demonstrates God's future plan of atonement for Israel and His removal of their sins. This future atonement will fall on a coming Day of Atonement.

The Day of Atonement thus pictures the full and complete atonement offered by the Lord Jesus Christ. That atonement redeems, satisfies, reconciles, and cleanses the sinner from the effects of his sin. For individuals, nations, and inanimate objects it makes them useful for God's service. Never forget that "the idea of cleansing is the main lesson in the Feast of Atonement" (Strauss 96).

The Application of Atonement

Aside from mentioning the normal yearly observance of the Day of Atonement, history records no other events connected with this feast. Even the recurrent agricultural theme fails on this occasion. Like the Feast of Trumpets, this feast signifies a future national event. Dwight Pentecost, citing Ryrie in support, sees a future time of salvation and ties it to the nation's restoration to the land.

> The sequence of events set up by the prophet [Jer. 32:37, 40-41] is that Israel will first be regathered and restored to the land and then will experience the blessings of the new covenant in the land. History records no such sequence. God cannot fulfill the covenant until Israel is regathered as a nation. Her complete restoration is demanded by the new covenant, and this has not yet taken place in the history of the world. . . . Fulfillment of the prophecies requires the regathering of all Israel, their spiritual rebirth, and the return of Christ. (Walvoord II:120)

The return of Christ is crucial to these happenings (Romans 11:26-27). Micah 4:1-6 relates that all of these things will happen in the "*last days,*" and will include the re-gathering and restoration of Israel (v. 6). Alva McClain states that while "'in the last days,' as used in the context of Micah 4, certainly refers to eschatological time, the prophecies of Israel's restoration cannot be regarded as fulfilled by any partial restorations in the past" (McClain 151). Further, Ezekiel, speaking of the same national event says,

> *And I will make them one nation in the land upon the mountains of Israel; and one king shall be king to them all; and they shall*

be no more two nations, neither shall they be divided into two kingdoms any more at all:

Ezekiel 37:22

Christ's return will bring about the re-unification of Israel, a process that will continue throughout the Millennium. Thus, the "covenant will be realized in the millennial age" (Walvoord II:121).

The re-gathering of Israel represents "one of the major themes of prophetic Scripture, beginning with the writings of Moses (Deut.30:1-3) and reaching its climax in the minor prophets. Yet the sole notice given to it in many theological works is a denial that it will ever be fulfilled" (McClain 198). To deny Israel's future in the Millennium denies the clear teaching of Scripture. Lehman Strauss speaks not only of the re-gathering but also says that "there is both a future gathering and a future glory for Israel" in the Millennium (106). Only God could accomplish a true spiritual re-gathering and restoration to glory for Israel. The Feast of Trumpets begins the process of restoration and the Day of Atonement completes it. 'Israel's greatest need is a spiritual one. Possessing the land and having protection from their enemies cannot solve the nation's biggest problem. Before the nation can enjoy lasting peace and protection, repentance and cleansing from sin are imperative' (Strauss 96).

Ten days intervene between these two feasts, days that the Jewish people see as a time for heart searching, confession, repentance, and reconciliation (Donin 247). They call these periods the "Ten Days of Repentance" and the "Sabbath which falls during this ten-day period is known as *Shabbat Teshuvah*, the Sabbath of Repentance, or as *Shabbat Shuvah*, the Sabbath of Return." When Jewish people greet each other during these days, they say, "May the final seal be for good." Their greeting expresses the belief that Rosh Hashana and Yom Kippur are Days of Judgment (*Yom Hadin*) for all people (Donin 246). Even in their spiritual blindness, contemporary Jewish people often hold some of the views held by many Premillennial Biblical commentators who believe in a pre-Tribulation Rapture of the Church followed by seven years of judgment or Tribulation and ended by the literal physical second coming of Jesus Christ to the earth.

The Tribulation serves two primary functions. First, it provides a time of distinct judgment upon the world of the Gentile nations (Psalm 2:1-10; Isaiah 63:1-6; Joel 3:2-16; Zephaniah 3:8; Zechariah 14:1-3). Second, it restores Israel to its place in God's program and lays the groundwork for the coming Millennial kingdom in fulfillment of the Covenants. At the end of the Tribulation, the Lord Jesus Christ will come back to Jerusalem as He left it. *"Ye men of Galilee, why stand ye gazing up into heaven? This same Jesus which is taken up from you into heaven, shall so come in like manner as ye have seen him go into heaven"* (Acts 1:11). He must physically come back in order to begin His earthly, thousand-year theocracy.

God's physical presence on the earth requires Israel's atonement (cleansing) as a nation in order to prevent it from "contaminating" its God. Once cleaned as a nation, Israel is free to enter the Millennium. Ezekiel mentions a national conversion in chapter 36. Such a conversion is necessary since no unsaved person may enter the Millennium. The Second Advent will witness this national conversion (all true Israel), thus fulfilling the national covenants during the age of the Messiah's reign (Pentecost 507). Romans 11:26-27, Isaiah 1:27, 4:3-4, Jeremiah 23:6, 24:7, 31:33-34, Ezekiel 11:19, 36:25-26, Joel 2:32, Micah 7:18-19, Zephaniah 3:12-13, and Zechariah 13:1, 9 all support this interpretation.

The cleansing or atonement of the nation enables it to enter the Millennium in God's holy service. The Passover Lamb redeemed: *"Purge out therefore the old leaven, that ye may be a new lump, as ye are unleavened. For even Christ our passover is sacrificed for us"* (1 Corinthians 5:7). Christ's death on the Cross propitiated (or satisfied) God. Now comes the great reconciliation and cleansing at the Day of Atonement: *"Behold, he cometh with clouds; and every eye shall see him, and they also which pierced him: and all kindreds of the earth shall wail because of him. Even so, Amen"* (Revelation 1:7). *"I saw in the night visions, and, behold, one like the Son of man came with the clouds of heaven, and came to the Ancient of days, and they brought him near before him"* (Daniel 7:13). At last, the cleansing, prophesied by Ezekiel, comes to Israel:

> *And I will pour upon the house of David, and upon the inhabitants of Jerusalem, the spirit of grace and of supplications: and they shall*

look upon me whom they have pierced, and they shall mourn for him, as one mourneth for his only son, and shall be in bitterness for him, as one that is in bitterness for his firstborn.

Zechariah 12:10

Notice that God pours out His grace, for Israel has done nothing to merit reconciliation to Him. Only through God's grace will Israel repent of its sin and be cleansed.

Never lose sight of the fact that the Tribulation is both a Gentile and a Jewish event. The events taking place on the earth during the Tribulation **do not** concern the Church. The Church, all true believers who have individually recognized Jesus of Nazareth as their Messiah or Christ, received atonement through the Cross, each member receiving atonement at the time of his or her repentance and acceptance of Christ (salvation). However, no such event has yet occurred in Israel's national life. Until such recognition and acceptance comes, the atonement of Christ's blood will not apply to **national** Israel. In order to be consistent with the teaching revealed in the atonement and in the Feasts, the central focus of the Second Coming **must** be Israel and the kingdom. Remember, the Feasts primarily apply **only** to historical events related to Israel. Thus, the atonement taught in Leviticus 16 and 23 must apply directly to national Israel. "For the children of Israel the Day of Atonement was the greatest event of the entire year. On that day forgiveness and cleansing from sin were not merely for individuals, but for all the sins of the whole nation" (Strauss 97).

The Day of Atonement: A Summation

The doctrine of the substitutionary atonement has far-reaching applications for both Israel and the Church. When Jesus Christ died upon the Cross, He performed a great transaction in that He made atonement available to all (individuals or nations) who would accept it. Regardless of the fact that Christ provides sufficient atonement for all men, only those who recognize Him as Savior benefit from the atonement that He offers. The man who sees no need for cleansing cannot experience atonement's cleansing action. While the true Church teaches and understands this idea, Israel, in its temporary national blindness, has not yet experienced this understanding. Keeping in mind that the Feasts of the LORD apply primarily to Israel, we recognize that Israel must eventually accept cleansing as a nation.

The Day of Atonement is the great feast on which the Lord Jesus Christ will apply His atonement to Israel on a national level. The nation will then recognize Him as its true Messiah. In Zechariah 12:11-14 the Scriptures make it clear that each individual person, Jewish or Gentile, must choose Christ as Lord and Savior. The same text also shows that God will bring about repentance on a national scale and cleanse Israel on that day. God will bring about the great reconciliation and restoration between Himself and Israel. Israel will then know full rest, *shabat shabbaton*, from its struggles involving the world, the Covenant, and its relationship to God. S. H. Kellogg says of the Day of Atonement that

> . . . it expressed in a far higher degree than any other festival the other sabbatic idea of complete restoration brought in through expiation for sin. This was indeed the central thought of the whole ceremonial of the day, --the complete removal of all those sins of the nation which stood between them and God, and hindered complete restoration to God's favor. (464)

Through atonement, God makes the nation clean from sin to such an extent that it can enter the Millennium in His service and in fulfillment of His covenant promise. "On that day of Israel's national atonement, the iniquity of the land shall be removed 'in one day' (Zechariah 3:9)" (Kellogg 108). Further, after the national atonement, Israel will experience full and complete access to the Lord, resulting in total fellowship with the Messiah, the Lord Jesus Christ, as He reigns over them. The application of atonement will continue throughout the Millennium, for sin will still be present in the Millennium. The sin nature will not, as yet, be eradicated, and new people (who need atonement for their sins) will be born. God will provide for them as well: "*In that day there shall be a fountain opened to the house of David and to the inhabitants of Jerusalem for sin and for uncleanness*" (Zechariah 13:1).

Cleansing and purification apply to inanimate objects of worship as well. Sacrifices will not expiate sin (Christ paid it all); rather, they will cleanse the objects from sin's taint. Atonement extended to inanimate objects goes no further. God's holiness demands holiness and cleanliness while He reigns in the world. Remember, He is holy and cannot be tarnished by sin.

In addition to its application to Israel, God must also apply atonement to the world since sin has altered the material universe.

> *For we know that the whole creation groaneth and travaileth in pain together until now. And not only they, but ourselves also, which have the firstfruits of the Spirit, even we ourselves groan within ourselves, waiting for the adoption, to wit, the redemption of our body.*
>
> Romans 8:22,23

In the Millennium, God will restore the earth back to its Garden of Eden state (Isaiah 35), and it too will know cleansing.

As the Musaf prayer expresses, Israel's only healing can come from the Messiah. At the end of the day of Yom Kippur, a final, single, long blast of the shofar sounds closing the feast. This feast does not mark the conclusion of God's plan, however. Someday, God will bring about the full application of the atonement, finished on the Cross, but not yet applied to creation and nations.

CHAPTER 9:
THE FEAST OF TABERNACLES

Feast of Tabernacles

And ye shall rejoice before the Lord your God seven days.

Leviticus 23:40b

Many years ago, my family and I went camping in the Kettle Moraine hills of Wisconsin. I remember walking at night on a hillside above our camp and seeing how our campfire lighted up the area around it. What a contrast to the surrounding darkness! The campfire radiated light and clearly showed me the way back to camp. During the days of the Feast of Tabernacles, the great candelabras of the Temple court would have lighted the dark world around it with greater intensity. Lights, a significant feature of the Feast of Tabernacles, visually reflect the culmination of Israel's spiritual and agricultural year and add merriment to the feast's grand and joyful rejoicing. The rabbis, speaking for many, say, "He who has not seen Jerusalem during the Feast of Tabernacles does not know what rejoicing means" (Buksbazen

46). Josephus calls the Feast of Tabernacles the "most holy and most eminent" of the seven Feasts of the LORD (218). The many names of this feast reflect its eminence:

- **The Feast of Tabernacles (Leviticus 23:34)**
- **The Feast of Booths**
- **The Feast of Ingathering (Leviticus 23:39, Exodus 23:16; 34:22)**
- **The Thanksgiving Feast**
- *The* **Feast (John 7:37)**

Three times, God calls upon Israel to rejoice at this feast (Leviticus 23:40, Deuteronomy 16:14-15). Further, the Jewish prayer book stresses that this feast is the "season of our rejoicing, '*zman simhatainu*'" (Donin 251). Lehman Strauss believes that "it was the Lord's intention that this final feast be a time of great rejoicing" (117). Rejoicing culminates the spiritual year in Israel.

Israelites could not miss the central theme of rejoicing. For them the feast was the last feast of the year as well as the last Pilgrimage Feast. It also coincided with the final harvest. Significantly, the feast occurs in the Seventh Month, the number seven signifying totality, and thus completes the year's spiritual activities. Bracketed by two special Sabbaths, it links rejoicing with worship. These elements make the feast far more than a mere harvest celebration. Rather, the joy of worshipping "*before the Lord*" is the prime emphasis.

This emphasis, however, does not completely rule out an agricultural side to the event. In reality, all three Pilgrimage Feasts have spiritual and agricultural aspects. The first Pilgrimage Feast, Unleavened Bread, through its association with the start of the barley harvest, pictures the formation of God's theocracy in which He separated Israel from pagan Egypt. The second Pilgrimage Feast, Pentecost, associated with the start of the wheat harvest, pictures national, spiritual Judaism, sealed by the Covenant. Finally, the last Pilgrimage Feast, Tabernacles, through its connection with the completion of the final harvest, pictures God's termination of the Wilderness Period and the entrance of His people into the Promised Land.

The Feast of Tabernacles is, unquestionably, a complex event possessed of several different facets. Like all of the previous feasts, it has both a historical and a spiritual significance. Like the previous two feasts, the Feast of Trumpets and the Day of Atonement, it also has a

future fulfillment and historical significance. In order to understand the Feast of Tabernacles completely, we must examine each aspect of the feast and understand its contribution to the entire picture.

The Instructions for the Feast

God's main instructions for the Feast of Tabernacles (Leviticus 23:34-40) proclaim an eight-day feast with Sabbaths at the beginning and end of the period.

Speak unto the children of Israel, saying, The fifteenth day of this seventh month shall be the feast of tabernacles for seven days unto the LORD. On the first day shall be a holy convocation: ye shall do no servile work therein. Seven days ye shall offer an offering made by fire unto the LORD: on the eighth day shall be a holy convocation unto you; and ye shall offer an offering made by fire unto the LORD: it is a solemn assembly; and ye shall do no servile work therein. . . And ye shall take you on the first day the boughs of goodly trees, branches of palm trees, and the boughs of thick trees, and willows of the brook; and ye shall rejoice before the LORD your God seven days.

Notice that these verses do not emphasize the harvest. Rather, they emphasize worship by using such terms as "*holy convocation [miqra]*," "*no servile work*," and "*solemn assembly [aseret].*" *Miqra*, a synonym for *moed* (one of the Hebrew words for feast), articulates God's command for "an appointed worship gathering," where "the godly were to focus their time and effort on worship" (*TWOT* 811). All Israelites therefore had to make the pilgrimage to holy Jerusalem in obedience to God's "call."

In addition to the instructions of Leviticus 23, Deuteronomy 16:13-15 provides a second look at the feast from a different perspective. Unfortunately, the second set of instructions creates some potential confusion by specifying a different length for the feast (seven days instead of eight) and by giving the impression that the feast's emphasis is primarily agricultural.

Thou shalt observe the feast of tabernacles seven days, after that thou hast gathered in thy grain and thy wine: And thou shalt rejoice in thy feast, thou, and thy son, and thy daughter, and thy man servant, and thy maidservant, and the Levite, the stranger, *and the fatherless, and the widow, that are within thy gates. Seven days shalt thou keep a solemn feast unto the L*ORD *thy God in the place which the L*ORD *shall choose: because the L*ORD *thy God shall bless thee in all thine increase, and in all the works of thine hands, therefore thou shalt surely rejoice.*

Contemporary Jewish writers place great emphasis upon the agricultural aspect of the feast. They call it "the fall harvest festival" (Knoebel n.p.). Keil also treats the feast as "a feast of thanksgiving for the gathering in of the produce of the land" (*Pentateuch* 449). At first glance, we appear to have **two** feasts that share the same name, occur in the same space of time, and yet conflict in their emphases (historical/spiritual versus agricultural).

Arguing in favor of two coincidental yet distinct feasts is the fact that Deuteronomy speaks of a seven-day feast whereas Leviticus speaks of an eight-day feast. Since feasts do sometimes share the same space of time (First Fruits and Unleavened Bread for example), this interpretation is not without precedent. Arguing for a single feast is the fact that both passages call the feast by the same name, the Feast of Tabernacles. Further, both passages employ the term *moed*, which denotes divine appointments between God and His nation.

Comparison of Feast of Tabernacles Instructions								
Feast Day	1st	2nd	3rd	4th	5th	6th	7th	8th
Leviticus 23:34	Holy Convocation							
	Offering made by fire							
Leviticus 23:36								Holy Convocation ———— Offering
Deut. 16:13-15	Thou Shalt Rejoice Keep a Solemn Feast							

Figure 15 – Two Feasts?

144

Believing that God wrote the Scriptures without error and that the text that we have represents that infallible Word of God, we know that the two passages cannot contradict each other. Any interpretation of these two passages must harmonize the apparent discrepancies. Further, recall that all of the previous feasts teach spiritual truths of God: deliverance, sanctification, resurrection, salvation of both Jewish people and Gentiles, covenantal revival in Israel, and atonement. Any conclusions that we draw to help us to interpret the Feast of Tabernacles must be consistent with the structure and purposes of the other feasts.

Summing all of these facts together, we conclude that Leviticus 23 and Deuteronomy 16 speak of just **one** feast, the Feast of Tabernacles. Furthermore, the apparent differences are actually two converging themes that combine to form a complete picture that includes both historical/spiritual and future-looking aspects. The compatibility of the two passages rests on the understanding that Deuteronomy uses the **physical** harvest as an illustration of the **spiritual** truths taught in Leviticus. The agricultural aspect is not a hypocritical pagan means of gaining God's favor and graciousness for the next harvest. The ultimate purpose of the feast makes the agricultural aspect subservient to the historical/spiritual aspect. The harvest illustration points out not only God's care and provision but also God's faithfulness to provide and accomplish all that He has promised to Israel.

We resolve the confusion created by the eighth day mentioned in the Leviticus passage in the next chapter. As it turns out, its presence does not interfere with the seven days that the passages share in common. Since the eighth day is not connected with the agricultural side of the feast, the Deuteronomy passage omits it from its instructions. On the other hand, since the eighth day has historical/spiritual significance, the Leviticus passage includes it.

Passage in Bible	Feast Aspect Emphasized	Number of Days of Observance
Leviticus	Historical/Spiritual	8
Deuteronomy	Agricultural	7

Figure 16 – Two Feasts? No!

The Celebration of the Feast of Tabernacles

The idea of a spiritual pilgrimage reaches its zenith with this feast. From all over the world, Jewish men came to the feast (Deuteronomy 16:16) and appeared before the LORD. During New Testament times, God's command drew pilgrims from Media, Arabia, Persia, India, Italy, Spain, modern Crimea, and even from the banks of the Danube (*Life and Times* 390). The yearly pilgrimage to holy Jerusalem became a sort of "re-enactment" of the journey from pagan Egypt to the Promised Land.

The participants in the Feast of Tabernacles included all Jewish people and all Gentiles who were residents of Jewish cities. Deuteronomy 16:11 notes that these cities were ones *"where the LORD thy God hath chosen to place his name there."* Like the Feast of Pentecost, the Feast of Tabernacles provides for Gentiles. Despite the seeming openness of this feast, however, it was limited to Gentiles who lived in God's cities, a regulation whose symbolism undoubtedly has significance in the feast's future-looking aspect.

Upon his arrival on the first day of the feast, the pilgrim, acting on God's instructions, constructed a booth or tabernacle (temporary dwelling place) to serve as his lodging during the feast.

> *Ye shall dwell in booths seven days; all that are Israelites born shall dwell in booths: That your generations may know that I made the children of Israel to dwell in booths, when I brought them out of the land of Egypt: I am the LORD your God.*
>
> Leviticus 23:42,43

The booths served not only to remind the pilgrim of Israel's forty-year journey in the Wilderness with its accompanying lack of permanent dwellings but also to emphasize the nature of Israel's seemingly precarious existence during those years. No Jewish man could forget that God's provision of manna sustained the nation in the Wilderness. God designed this historical reminder to encourage a worshipful expression of gratitude toward Him and to remind Israel that it owed its existence to Him and thus its obedience as well.

God instructs Israel to have a Sabbath on the first day and a *"solemn assembly [asereth]"* on the last day of the feast (Leviticus 23:35-36, 39). While both days are Sabbaths (v. 39), and both call for the gathering of the nation (vv. 35, 39), only the last Sabbath is described as a "*solemn assembly.*" This distinction must have significance. In order to understand it, we must look closely at the meaning of the expression "*solemn assembly.*" Andrew Bonar translates it "solemn close" rather than the Authorized Version's "*solemn assembly*" (414). He bases his translation upon Joel 1:14: "*Hold the most solemn assembly you can, like the closing days in any of your feasts.*" Further, Josephus uses the Greek word *asarqa*, formed from *aseret*, to denote "close" (Bonar 414). The *Torah Commentary* notes that the Septuagint renders the expression *exodion* (from which we derive the English words "exodus" and "exit") or "finale, recessional." (*JPS Torah* 162). Therefore, "solemn close" or "finale" is probably the best translation for *asereth* in the context of Leviticus 23:36. If we accept this interpretation of the expression, the last Sabbath day of the Feast of Tabernacles is the "finale" of the feast. As we will see in the next chapter, the final Sabbath symbolizes a final event in history for Israel and for mankind.

Like those of the Feast of Unleavened Bread, the five days after the opening Sabbath were "half-holy" days in that the people could work and go about their normal activities. The seventh day and the eighth day (the final Sabbath), however, were special and included several events of great spiritual and symbolic significance.

On the first six days of the feast (the opening Sabbath and the five half-holy days), the priests formed a procession and encircled the altar singing "*O then, now work salvation, Lord, O Lord give prosperity*" (Psalm 118:25). On the seventh day, they circled the altar seven times as a remembrance of God's victory at Jericho. The idea behind this act was that God would directly bring down the walls of heathenism and the land would then lie open for His people to go in and possess.

Day	1st	2nd	3rd	4th	5th	6th	7th	8th
Events	Daily Sacrifices							
	Procession and Circle Altar Once							
							Procession Circle Altar 7 Times	
								Solemn Assembly
								Burn Booths

Figure 17 – Events of the Feast of Tabernacles

John 7 records some of the events of the seventh day of the feast (the day before the terminal Sabbath) in the time of Christ: "*Now the Jews' feast of tabernacles was at hand*" (v. 2). On this day the people gathered at the Temple site in Jerusalem. Many would go down to the pool of Siloam to witness the priestly feast procession from the pool to the Temple. A priest would carry two golden pint pitchers of water from the pool. At the same time, a second procession would begin in the Kidron Valley.

As they moved toward the Temple, the people would gather up willow branches and form a canopy under which the priests would proceed to the altar of burnt offerings. During the procession, trumpets would be blown. At the Water Gate (named for this ceremony), the priest bearing the water would enter as the trumpeters sounded three blasts. Since the people had to witness the next action, they would cry, "raise your hand." Standing before two silver basins, he would pour water into one and wine into the other. The Talmud records the water as symbolizing the pouring out of the Holy Spirit of God. The great Temple orchestra then began playing the Hallel (Psalms 113-118). During the performance the people would listen to the words sung by the choir and wave their *lulavs* (willow branches) toward the altar and recite, "*O give thanks to the Lord*" (Psalm 118:1), "*O work then now salvation Lord*" (Psalm 118:25*)*, "*O give thanks to the Lord*" (Psalm 118:29).

Pouring the water was just one part of the day's worship, however. The day began with the regular daily sacrifices, followed by additional sacrifices, and votive and free-will offerings. Then the people enjoyed a festive meal, followed by a study of the Law. At evening, the priests offered the regular sacrifices after which they poured the water by way of a climax. After dark, four golden candelabras lit the occasion, and the people joined in by holding lighted torches. Both Jewish people and Gentiles were allowed to be present in the Court of Women during the services.

Jewish tradition teaches that on the fifteenth day of Tishri, the pillar of cloud by day and the pillar of fire by night had first come to Israel to guide God's people to the Promised Land. The memory of the Shekinah lingered since the Temple site glowed for all to see on the night of the Great Feast, the Feast of Tabernacles. In our Lord's day, the following words were recited as the trumpets sounded: "Our fathers who were in this place, they turned their back upon the Sanctuary of the Lord and their faces toward the east, and they worshipped towards the rising sun, but as for us our eyes are towards the LORD (Sukk. v. 4)" (Edersheim 391). Clearly this recitation is an allusion to the days when the Shekinah Glory was forced to leave the Temple due to Israel's pagan worship (Ezekiel 8:1-18).

The entire ceremony looked to a future possession and peace for God's people. The songs, actions, and thoughts all focused on the coming Messiah and the peace that He would bring. This attitude of expectancy explains why on Palm Sunday (the Day of Preparation prior to the Passover) the people believed that Jesus was offering Himself as King and Messiah (Matthew 21:8-9; John 12:12-13). Realizing that the Feast of Tabernacles would one day herald the Messiah's entry into Jerusalem and yet ignoring the fact that the Feast of Tabernacles was still seven months away, they saw the occasion as that of the Messiah's promised coming. They based their erroneous conclusion on the special significance taught concerning the last day of the Feast of Tabernacles which they called "The Day of the Great Hosanna." On this occasion, they would sing the words of Psalm 118:24-27:

This is the day which the Lord hath made; we will rejoice and be glad in it. Save now, I beseech thee, O Lord: O Lord, I beseech thee, send now prosperity. Blessed be he that cometh in the name of the Lord: we have blessed you out of the house of the Lord, God is the Lord, which hath showed us light: bind the sacrifice with cords, even unto the horns of the altar. Thou art my God, and I will praise thee: though art my God, I will exalt thee.

Through this song, they testified to the future aspect of the Feast of Tabernacles and their expectation of a literal kingdom with a literal King, the Messiah, on that future day.

Interestingly, on a previous occasion during the seventh day of the Feast of Tabernacles, Jesus **did** rise to speak (John 7:37). Using the picture of the water ceremony, He cried, "*If any man thirst, let him come unto me, and drink, he that believeth on me, as the Scripture hath said, out of his belly shall the flow the rivers of living water.*" Here, He clearly proclaimed Himself as Messiah with these words. Earlier in the week, the people had been speculating that Jesus might be the Messiah (John 7:26). All of the signs and miracles pictured in Isaiah 35 seemed to point to Him. The people's speculation shows that they anticipated a literal Messiah. Thus, during the worship service of the seventh day, Jesus of Nazareth equated the living waters with Himself and offered Himself to Israel as the Messiah. Some recognized Him as such (John 7:41) while others disagreed, resulting in division (John7:43). Unfortunately, the leaders of the nation rejected Him and consequently led the people into rejection as well. This incident on the Feast of Tabernacles prefigures the future one to come. Clearly, by His offer, Jesus Christ linked the coming of the Messiah, the coming literal kingdom, and the coming peace and spiritual healing with the Feast of Tabernacles. By His testimony, this feast takes on a future aspect.

The eighth day, the final Sabbath, was the time of "*solemn assembly*" before the LORD, the "finale" of the feast. At the conclusion of the assembly, the people burned their booths and the pilgrims returned to their homes, an action whose symbolic significance will become apparent in the next chapter.

The Historical/spiritual Aspect of the Feast

Lehman Strauss places the historical/spiritual element in the forefront when he states that "Leviticus 23 projects more prophecy and presents more of God's plan for Israel than any other chapter we can call to mind. Step by step, from commencement to consummation, the divine purpose graphically unfolds" (13). Any explanation of the Feasts of Israel must consider the duality of the historical/spiritual (Leviticus 23:34-36) and agricultural (Leviticus 23:39) elements of all of the Feasts and of this feast in particular.

God's chosen symbol for this feast is the booth (*sukka*). During the Wilderness Period, the Israelites used both booths and tents. The tent was probably similar to the modern Bedouin tent. Tents served well during the actual journey. They could be easily raised prior to nightfall and easily packed for the journey the next day. Booths, however, required more effort to erect, necessitating a time-consuming gathering of available materials (*TWOT* 624). Thus, Israel used them only when it remained in one area for a sustained period of time. We must remember that Israel was not constantly on the move during the forty-year Wilderness Period. It undoubtedly remained in certain areas for short periods of temporary "residency."

The symbolism developed so far falls somewhat short of the full picture, however. Curiously, a number of interesting peculiarities emerge out of God's choice of the booth as the symbol of the feast. Since the tent is a more temporary structure than the booth, we might naturally wonder why God chose the former rather than the latter as the feast's representative image. Further, if the booths were to picture the transient and temporary nature of life in the Wilderness, we would expect them to be constructed in a way consistent with wilderness conditions (i.e. with poor quality materials). Instead, however, God instructs Israel to construct the booths of "*goodly trees, branches of palm trees, and the boughs of thick trees, and willows of the brook*" (Leviticus 23:40). Keil notes that these materials are hardly reminiscent of deprivation and difficulty: "Moreover, the booths used at this feast were not made of miserable shrubs of the desert, but of branches of fruit-trees, palms and thickly covered trees, the produce of the good and glorious land into which God had brought them" (*Pentateuch* 450). Contrary to our expectations, the booth materials serve as **poor** reminders of the Israelites' desert life.

Even this feast's relationship to the other feasts seems anomalous. If this feast exists solely as a remembrance of the wanderings that followed the Exodus, then we would expect to find it in the spring along with the other feasts associated with the times of the Exodus, the Wilderness Period, and the entry into the Promised Land. Logic therefore suggests that the Feast of Tabernacles should belong to the **first** cluster of feasts rather than to the **last**. Finally, the rejoicing associated with this feast seems at odds with the rigors of the Wilderness Period. Consequently, we must conclude that the booth symbolizes much more than just the Wilderness Period.

Keil offers a possible explanation by suggesting that "privation and want can never be an occasion of joy; rather its emphasis was to place vividly before the eyes of the future generations of Israel a memorial of the grace, care, and protection which God afforded to His people in the great and terrible wilderness (Deut. viii. 15)" (*Pentateuch* 450). Merrill Unger agrees: "The booth in Scripture is not an image of privation and misery, but of protection, preservation, and shelter from heat, storm, and tempest (Psa. 27:5; 31:20; Isa. 4:6)" (359). Booths serve "as a defense both against the heat of the sun, and also against wind and rain (Ps. xxxi, 21; Isa. Iv. 6; Jonah iv. 5)" (*Pentateuch* 449).

Perhaps W. G. Moorehead comes closest to a proper emphasis by treating the booth as a teaching tool for the Jewish people as well as for all true Believers (238). In the case of the Jewish people of the past, the booth taught them that the world was not their home. They were to see themselves as wanderers, strangers, and pilgrims who had no permanent abiding place. Instead, they were to look for the city that has foundations and whose builder is God. Their present home, a frail booth, will soon be dissolved, but God's people await their heavenly building (238).

Warren Wiersbe sees a further historical/spiritual significance in the symbol of the booths. They were a historical reminder to Israel of the contrast between the period of wandering during which they lived in temporary dwellings and the state of permanency in the Promised Land (110). The spiritual significance prefigures the coming kingdom of God upon the earth following the return of the Messiah (Zechariah 12:10-13:1, Isaiah 35, Luke 1:67-80) (111) when on "that grand day . . . God will raise up the fallen booth of David (Amos 9:11) and give shelter to his repentant, redeemed, and regathered people (Isa. 4:6)" (*TWOT* 624).

These interpretations when combined together harmonize fully with God's purposes and with the Scriptures. First, the feast is a historical reminder of the Wilderness Period along with its state of transience and total dependence upon God's provision. At the end of the journey, God fulfilled His promise by bringing Israel into the Promised Land. The last feast of the year therefore symbolizes the completed historical journey.

Second, the feast teaches a spiritual truth connected with the historical event and also points to a future fulfillment: "*But now they desire a better country, that is, a heavenly: wherefore God is not ashamed to be called their God: for he hath prepared for them a city*" (Hebrews 11:16). Abraham did not find the "*city*" but only a "*tabernacle*" (Hebrews 11:9-10). The adult generation of Israel did not find a "city," for, as Hebrews 3 explains, those who came out of Egypt could not enter "*his rest*" because of their unbelief. Finally, Jesus Christ spoke of a future "*rest*": "*There remaineth therefore a rest* [Sabbath rest for-literally] *to the people of God*" (Hebrews 4:9). The fulfillment of the promise is yet to come; in fact, that fulfillment is linked to the Gospel (Hebrews 4:1-3). Thus, the journey in this temporary world continues to this day for all who await a Sabbath rest.

The word "*rest,*" *sabbatismos sabbatismos*, occurs uniquely in Hebrews 4:9. Its uniqueness parallels the use of *shabbaton* in connection with the feasts of the Seventh Month. Homer Kent points out that it "is . . . different from the word used for 'rest' elsewhere" (*Hebrews* 84). Joseph Thayer defines the word as "the blessed rest from toils and troubles looked for in the age to come by the true worshippers of God and true Christians" (565). The uniqueness of this word, written primarily to the Jewish people of AD 60, suggests its familiarity to the people of that time (Alford IV:81). Thomas Rodgers points out "this is not future salvation rest. This is not faith rest. This is a future Sabbath rest" (24). He explains that both rabbis and Christians recognize Genesis 2:2 as foreseeing this rest: "God's Sabbath rest is the type of some future rest to come, a cessation from labor, some permanency with God Himself" (24). For Israel the entrance into the Promised Land was a preview, though incomplete, of the coming day of true spiritual rest in God's Heaven.

Even today, man has not found a permanent, secure, and eternal "*rest*" in this world. Like the memorial of the Feast of Trumpets, Tabernacles also serves as a memorial. It causes a recollection of past and present facts that, in turn, results in an action: a desire for a future "*rest.*" Through this desire man can recognize his total dependence upon God for his eternity, or he can reject the concept and face a Godless eternity. Thus, this feast points to a fitting "completion" of the journey of life. It does not recall the wanderings between Passover and First Fruits only; rather, it reminds mankind of the temporary, transient nature of this world from Passover to Tabernacles. Since this world has not yet been transformed, it is well for us as Believers to remember "*our citizenship is in heaven, from which also we eagerly wait for a Savior, the Lord Jesus Christ*" (Philippians 3:20). Therefore, the booths symbolize the past in Israel's historical journey, the present spiritual state of longing for "*rest,*" and the future in which "the booth . . . exhibited the scene of a world clad in rich, luxuriant verdure - men dwelling in peace, and sending up songs of praise amid every token of fresh and lively joy" (Bonar 411). Because the "*rest*" has not come and because the writer of Hebrews speaks in the context of Abraham and of the Covenant, we conclude that this feast must have a prophetic or future purpose as well.

Having examined the historical/spiritual significance of the feast and having seen that it must have a future significance as well, we must examine the agricultural side of the feast in order to complete the picture and to connect it to the two previous Pilgrimage Feasts.

The Agricultural Connection

While food on the table is a prime concern to many, spiritual matters viewed from the perspective of eternity take on greater importance, and daily needs pale in comparison. In the Scriptures the harvest is a figure of judgment in Jeremiah 51:33, Hosea 6:11, Joel 3:13, and Revelation 14:15. It is a figure of grace in Jeremiah 8:20 and a period of time for people to receive the Gospel in Matthew 9:37-38 and John 4:35 (Unger 457). The Scripture uses harvests as illustrations of the more important spiritual concepts of life.

The Lord Jesus Christ states that "*the harvest is the end of the world; and the reapers are the angels*" (Matthew 13:39). Further, those who "*offend*" and do "*iniquity*" are cast into a furnace of fire (Matthew

13:41-42). A second harvest element, "*sheaves*," appears eight times in the Bible. Except for references in the books of Ruth (2:7, 15) and Nehemiah (13:15), all references to the word "*sheaves*" refer to men involved in a figurative harvest. Even the prophetic sheaves of Joseph's dream (Genesis 37:7) and the sheaves of the feast hymn recorded in Psalm 126:6 (Perowne II:349) are actually symbolic of a spiritual harvest (Spurgeon II:77). Micah 4:12 speaks of the harvest at the end of the age when God will "*harvest*" men. Similar examples appear in Psalm 129:7 and Amos 2:13. Because of the Scriptures' extensive use of harvests as a figure of spiritual ingathering, we believe that the harvest aspect of the Feast of Tabernacles pictures an ongoing harvest of God's people culminating in the final harvest at the end of the age. After the final harvest is gathered in, the eternal rest of the "*new heavens and new earth*" begins.

The agricultural aspect of this feast acts as a supportive role, pointing to the main figure of eventual "*rest*" with the permanence symbolized by the end of booth dwelling. For "the origin and true signification of the feast of Tabernacles are not to be sought for in this natural allusion to the blessing of the harvest, but the dwelling in booths was the principal point in the feast" (*Pentateuch* 449). Victor Buksbazen summarizes: "The prophetic message of the Feast of Tabernacles is that there is shelter in the Tabernacle of God under the wings of the Shekinah glory, for the Jew first, and also the Gentile nations" (49). The two aspects of the Feast of Tabernacles, historical/spiritual and agricultural, converge into the important doctrinal teaching concerning the future significance of the Feast of Tabernacles, the end of this age and the eternal fellowship with God and rest for His elect.

The Future Aspect of the Feast

Of necessity we must verify that the Scriptures support such a future-looking aspect of the feast. Furthermore, such an interpretation must harmonize with the structure and symbolism developed in the other feasts.

In Chapter 4 we pointed out that the Feast of Unleavened Bread, a seven-day period of time starting and ending with Sabbaths, symbolizes the process of sanctification in a Believer's life. The Sabbaths at each end symbolize the Believer's necessary passivity in the positional and final sanctification phases of the process during which only God can act. Similarly, the five days between the Sabbaths symbolize the active portion of a Believer's life during which he grows and experiences progressive sanctification. Since the Feast of Tabernacles shares a very similar structure, we should look for a similar pattern in its symbolism.

A search of the Scriptures performed in a literal, historical, and grammatical hermeneutic reveals a pattern that harmonizes with the previously developed patterns and also addresses the need for a future fulfillment of the word "*rest*." If the Feasts truly picture events for the literal nation of Israel and its history and no "*rest*" now exists, then there must be a **future** historical and spiritual "*rest*" for the nation. The thousand-year reign of Christ, described in Revelation 20:4 and known as the Millennium, meets these conditions:

> *And I saw thrones, and they sat upon them, and judgment was given unto them: and I saw the souls of them that were beheaded for the witness of Jesus, and for the word of God, and which had not worshipped the beast, neither his image, neither had received his mark upon their foreheads, or in their hands; and they lived and reigned with Christ a thousand years.*

John adds an account of a future scene that would take place after the *"great tribulation"* (v. 14) at the Great Feast:

> *After this, I beheld, and lo, a great multitude, which no man could number, of all nations, and kindreds, and people, and tongues, stood before the throne, and before the Lamb, clothed with white robes, and palms in their hands; and cried with a loud voice, saying, salvation to our God which sitteth upon the throne, and unto the Lamb.*
>
> Revelation 7:9-10

This Lamb is the one who "*shall feed them and shall lead them unto living fountains of waters*" (Revelation 7:17). The allusions clearly point back to God's care during life in the Wilderness and also point forward to the promised messianic kingdom mentioned in Zechariah 12 and 13.

Pre-millennialists believe that Jesus Christ will return to the earth following a seven-year period of unique tribulation upon the earth (Matthew 24:21, Revelation 2:22; 7:14) and then reign for a thousand years in a literal kingdom. The Millennium and its surrounding events fit the symbolism developed in the Feast of Tabernacles.

The feast includes future history as well as past, for it is a "shadow" of the coming day when the Lord Jesus Christ shall be revealed as both the Lamb slain for His people and the King Who shall rule from the throne. The fact that the Jewish people of the Lord's day clearly associated this feast with the Messiah conclusively connects a future Feast of Tabernacles to a future, literal Israel and a future Kingdom. It is clear that the first Sabbath of the feast could well portray the "*rest*" for the earth from war and tribulation. The intermediate days of the feast symbolize the peace of the thousand-year reign of Christ. We will leave the significance of the final Sabbath for the next chapter.

Additional Millennial Connections

The Jewish people of New Testament times added two additional ceremonies to the feast beyond those specified by the Mosaic instructions: the water-pouring ceremony and the lighting ceremony. Later still, they added a ninth day, called Simchath Torah, meaning "Rejoicing over the Law" to the feast (Buksbazen 56). We must consider these additions in order to understand the full ramifications of the feast in its Millennial context.

Jesus Christ recognized and observed the two added elements without criticism. Indeed, He actually utilized them to make significant proclamations concerning Himself. Speaking in response to the closing words of Psalm 118, part of the Hallel, recited on the seventh day of the feast, He made a Messianic claim, proclaiming Himself to be the salvation of Israel. "*If any man thirst, let him come unto me, and drink. He that believeth on me, as the scripture hath said, out of his belly shall flow rivers of living water*" (John 7:37-38).

During the illumination ceremony of the Temple on the night before the morning of the eighth day, He proclaimed, "*I am the light of the world: he that followeth me shall not walk in darkness, but shall have the light of life*" (John 8:12). In this declaration He proclaimed Himself as sent from God. Further, He said that "*Your father Abraham rejoiced to see my day: and he saw it, and was glad*" (John 8:56). Next, He stated that He was God, the "*I AM*" (John 8:58). The response of the people (v. 59) indicates that they well understood His claims. Their expectations showed that they understood that the Messianic King would be proclaimed one day at the Feast of Tabernacles. For this reason many speculated that Jesus of Nazareth was the Messiah.

At the Transfiguration, Peter demonstrated the same association of the Messiah with the feast. He believed that the Messiah had come and was about to found the Millennial Kingdom. He believed that the event fulfilled the prophecy of Zechariah 14:16,

> *And it shall come to pass, that every one that is left of all the nations which came against Jerusalem shall even go up form year to year to worship the King, the LORD of hosts, and to keep the feast of tabernacles.*

This prophecy declared Israel's covenant kingdom and its king, the Messiah. To demonstrate his belief, Peter offered to build the booths of the Feast of Tabernacles, one for the Lord Jesus, one for Moses, and one for Elijah.

Finally, the people of Israel responded in a similar manner on Palm Sunday. Here too, the Lord presented Himself to Israel as its King. The people, believing that the king had come to take his throne, took the palms, an accompaniment to the Feast of Tabernacles, and proclaimed the coming of the King of Israel. "*Blessed be the King that cometh in the name of the Lord: peace in heaven and glory in the highest*" (Luke 19:38). These two historical events show that the people understood the link between the Feast of Tabernacles and the Messianic Kingdom and were eagerly awaiting both.

The Millennial Symbolism Explained

Bringing all of these purposes, pictures, and concepts together results in one clear teaching of the Feast of Tabernacles. The seven days of the Feast of Tabernacles represent the Millennial Kingdom with the Lord Jesus Christ as its King and reigning upon the earth in fellowship with people (recognizing that this group will include some, born later, who are not righteous). "This last feast on God's prophetic calendar points to the earthly reign of Israel's Messiah, Our Lord Jesus Christ" (Strauss 123).

The first Sabbath on the first day of the feast pictures rest for God's righteous people coming out of the Great Tribulation and entering the Millennial Kingdom. The righteous will include both Jewish people and Gentiles. "*And in that day there shall be a root of Jesse* [a descendent, the Lord Jesus Christ]*, which shall stand for an ensign of the people; to it shall the Gentiles seek: and his rest shall be glorious*" (Isaiah 11:10). Christ's reign will include "*rest*" for the earth and its creatures (Isaiah 11:1-10) as well as for mankind. In a direct allusion to the lighting ceremony of the Feast of Tabernacles and the Lord's declaration on the seventh day of the feast (John 7), Isaiah writes, "*The people that walked in darkness have seen a great light; they that dwell in the land of the shadow of death, upon them hath the light shined*" (Isaiah 9:2).

The days between the first and the eighth days represent the period of the age when "Israel shall enter into her kingdom. . . . a time of great rejoicing" (Wiersbe 94). This period of time will include worship and glorifying "*before the LORD your God seven days*" (Leviticus 23:40). During this period additional people will be born who will need salvation, thus necessitating a final harvest.

The last Sabbath, the final day of the feast, symbolizes the next age, the New Heavens and the New Earth. Only after this final consummation and new beginning can the true elect, Jewish and Gentile Believers find true, complete, final "*rest*." The futuristic significance of this feast is strengthened by the fact that this feast is the only one mentioned in the millennial passages of the Scriptures.

We might naturally wonder why the Feast of Tabernacles stands out as the key symbol of the Millennial Kingdom. Although we believe that all of the feasts will be observed during the Millennium, only this particular feast carries with it a judicial ordinance requiring attendance in Jerusalem each year (Zechariah 14:16-19). Further, many events in the Millennial Kingdom parallel the events of the Feast of Tabernacles.

All the peoples of the earth, not just Israelites, will be welcomed to the city of Jerusalem to worship the King. Men will travel from all points of the compass for the yearly observance. For on that day, the

King will "*stand . . . upon the mount of Olives, which is before Jerusalem on the east*" (Zechariah 14:4) just as the people anticipated in the time of Christ. As Jesus Christ taught at a past Feast of Tabernacles, healing will pour forth to the world to bring rest from illness and suffering as the "*living waters shall go out from Jerusalem*" (v. 8). Jerusalem shall be at peace ("*rest*"): "*there shall be no more utter destruction; but Jerusalem shall be safely inhabited*" (v. 11). All will be in a state of holiness: "*Yea, every pot in Jerusalem and in Judah shall be holiness unto the LORD of hosts; and all they that sacrifice shall come and take of them, and seethe therein: and in that day there shall be no more the Canaanite in the house of the Lord of host*" (v. 21). As Jesus Christ taught at the lighting ceremony on the Feast of Tabernacles mentioned in John 7, the "*city had no need of the sun, neither of the moon, to shine in it: for the glory of God did illuminate it, and the Lamb is the light thereof*" (Revelation 21:23). The feast with all its brilliance from the candelabras could only hint at the greatest Light of all, the King of kings and Lord of lords, Jesus Christ, the Messiah.

Isaiah 9:6, prophesying of the Messiah, mentions that "*The government shall be upon his shoulder.*" No Messiah has yet come to rule over the kingdom of Israel; thus the events mentioned in the passage are yet to come. John, speaking of this coming day says,

> *After this I beheld, and, lo, a great multitude, which no man could number, of all nations, and kindreds, and people, and tongues, stood before the throne, and before the Lamb, clothed with white robes, and palms [the materials used to build the booths] in their hands: And cried with a loud voice, saying salvation [Hosanna] to our God which sitteth upon the throne, and unto the Lamb.*
> Revelation 7:9,10

Isaiah speaks further of the day: "*And the ransomed of the LORD shall return, and come to Zion with songs and everlasting joy upon their heads: they shall obtain joy and gladness, and sorrow and sighing shall flee away*" (Isaiah 35:10). All of the elements mentioned in connection with the Feast of Tabernacles, the joy, the water, the light, the peace, the healing, and the permanence of the feast, will find fulfillment when the prophesies are fulfilled in the Millennial Kingdom.

God called the Tabernacle of the Wilderness Period the *"tent of appointment [moed]"* in Numbers 10:3. In Chapter 1 we defined a *moed* as a God-ordained appointment with His people. They were to gather at the pilgrimage, *hag*, to honor God at the place and time specified by Him. The pilgrimage of history culminates in the gathering of the peoples and nations at the start of the Millennium. The Feasts, consummated by the Feast of Tabernacles, are the ultimate time for God's people to give Him the honor that is His due, the honor owed the One Who fulfilled His covenant promise and now reigns as King of kings. No other event of human history can be pictured by anything approaching the Feast of Tabernacles. The day of temporary existence and habitation ends, and the Millennium begins. The Millennium, however, is really just the end of the beginning.

Figure 18 – Tabernacles Through the Years

Scripturally Commanded Events of the Feast of Tabernacles								
Feast Day	1st	2nd	3rd	4th	5th	6th	7th	8th
Date Tishri	15	16	17	18	19	20	21	22
Instruction in Scripture	Holy Convocation	Chol Ha Moed [Half-holy days]						Holy Convocation
Designation	Sabbath							Solemn Assembly
Israel's Observance of the Feasts								
Old Testament Israel	Pillar of fire/cloud appeared							
A Typical Feast Observance During Christ's Childhood	Take boughs and construct	Live in Booths						Burn Booths
	Daily Sacrifices							
	Procession and circle the altar once						Procession circle altar 7 times	
							Festive meal	
							Study Law	
							Wave Lulavs	
							Water Pouring	

	Jesus Speaks at Temple — Offers Self as Messaih	Jesus Again Speaks to Israel John 8
Autumn Before Spring of Crucifixion		
	Millennial Kingdom	New Heavens and Earth
Israel's Future Symbolized by Tabernacles	Start of Millennium	

CHAPTER 10:
THE JUBILEE

He which testifieth these things saith, Surely I come quickly. Amen.
Even so come, Lord Jesus.

Revelation 22:20

My daughter and I love jigsaw puzzles. We spend hours finding just the right piece. Rather than a frustration, we find it very satisfying to fit the pieces together. We always start in the same way. First, we find the pieces with straight edges that make up the borders of the puzzle. Once they are fitted into place, we move on to the areas in between the borders. Inevitably, there is some area with missing pieces. We look at the remaining pieces and say, "How can they fit?" Over the last twenty years, I have been able to put together many of the pieces of the "Feast" puzzle. Yet, until recently, there remained one area of the puzzle with several missing pieces. Whenever I taught Leviticus 23, I was always careful to avoid verse 3.

Six days shall work be done: but the seventh day is the sabbath of rest, a holy convocation; ye shall do no work therein: it is the sabbath of the LORD in all your dwellings.

Clearly, the verse refers the Sabbath in relation to the Creation account of Genesis, so I felt that it belonged in Genesis, not in Leviticus. Have you ever notice how expositors often quickly pass over verses for which they have no explanation? I too have been guilty of this very practice. For me, Leviticus 23:3 was a puzzle piece from some other puzzle. I placed it aside with two other pieces that just "didn't fit."

One of those other pieces was the eighth day of the Feast of Tabernacles. Some writers include it as part of the feast while others claim that it is part of a separate, concurrent feast. Who is right? The problem remained unanswered until I found that the eighth day puzzle piece matched the Leviticus 23:3 piece.

The third, crucial piece turned up when a pastor in the Bahamas called me and asked me to tell him about the Jubilee and the way in which it fits with the Feasts. I told him that it was a separate event. He replied, "Check your text!" A study of the context of the Jubilee (Leviticus 25) and the Feasts (Leviticus 23) showed that they did, in fact, belong together. What a surprise for me! I had missed this connection for years. Now I had three pieces beautifully linked, and I only had to place them in the puzzle to complete the total picture of the Feasts of Israel.

The First Piece of the Puzzle: Creation Among the Feasts?

In Leviticus 23:2 God tells Moses to "*Speak unto the children of Israel, and say unto them, concerning the feasts of the LORD.*" With this verse God begins the instructions for the Feasts of Israel. Yet the very next verse seems to regress back to Genesis 2:2. The pattern of six days of work followed by a seventh day of rest reminds the reader of the days of Creation. After all, the weekly pattern of work followed by the Sabbath "is a creation ordinance (Ex. 20:8-11)" (*New Bible Dictionary* 1042). After this apparently anomalous insertion, verse 4 returns to the Feasts. Do these verses have something in common, or has God gone off on a tangent?

Anomaly of Leviticus 23:3	
Leviticus 23:1-2	Introduction–Feasts of the Lord
Leviticus 23:3	Six Days of Creation and Rest
Leviticus 23:4-44	Feast Instructions Begin

Figure 19 – An Anomaly in Scripture?

This book demonstrates that the Feasts picture either past or a future "mountain-top" experience for national Israel. All directly tie in to Israel's history. Additionally, each feast pictures a great spiritual truth of God as He deals with mankind in general. The puzzling part of Leviticus 23:1-4 is that the passage gives the impression that God is speaking of two distinct subjects, Creation and the Feasts. Since the Creation comes well before the history of Israel, its presence in this passage creates the same effect as a casual reference to the Garden of Eden would create in a book about American history. It seems out of place in a context focusing upon Israel's national history.

Parenthetically, the third verse of Leviticus 23 injects a subject that occurred long before the beginning of national Israel. Interestingly, the last feast, the Feast of Tabernacles records both the conclusion of Israel's history as well as that of the present earth's. If the teaching of the Feasts leads to the end of the age, could it in some way also point back to the beginning as well?

Scripture	Leviticus 23:3	Leviticus 23:5	Leviticus 23:39-44
Creation's History	Beginning		End
Israel's National History	————	Beginning	End
Feast - Symbol	????	Feast of Passover	Feast of Tabernacles

Figure 20 – History in the Feasts?

God does, in fact, use the Feasts to teach a significant truth instituted in the Garden of Eden. This truth comes out in Acts 3:21:

Repent ye therefore, and be converted, that your sins may be blotted out, when the times of refreshing shall come from the presence of the Lord; and he shall send Jesus Christ, which before was preached unto you: whom the heaven must receive until the times of restitution of all things, which God hath spoken by the mount of all his holy prophets since the world began.

Acts 3:19-21

Here, Peter, speaking at the Temple, discusses Israel's national rejection of the Messiah (vv. 12-18) and then extends the opportunity to "*repent*" and be "*converted*" (v. 19). The result of Israel's repentance would be the initiation of the "*times of refreshing* [which] *shall come from the presence of the Lord*" (v. 19). Peter makes two important points. First, the repentance of the nation will bring in "*times of refreshing,*" and secondly, such refreshment comes from "*the presence of the Lord.*" At this point in Church history, the "*times of refreshing*" are still in the future, and Jesus Christ is at the right hand of the Father in heaven (Acts 7:55). Necessary to the "*times of refreshing*" is the coming of the Lord. God also says that this event and these times have been prophesied "*since the world began.*" This passage links the consummation of the age with the Creation, just as the Feasts apparently do. Peter is not the first to speak of the coming refreshment.

Simeon (Luke 2:25-32) had looked for just such a time, for he had been "*waiting for the consolation of Israel*" (v. 25). The Hebrew world viewed the "*times of refreshing,*" "*restitution,*" and "*consolation of Israel*" as synonymous terms. Simeon declared the baby Jesus to be the means of fulfilling the prophecy spoken by Isaiah:

I the LORD have called thee in righteousness, and will hold thine hand, and will keep thee, and give thee for a covenant of the people, for a light of the Gentiles.

Isaiah 42:6

We find that in Isaiah's passage, he also speaks of Creation (v. 5), the redemption of Israel (43:1), the payment of ransom (43:3), the people God formed for Himself (43:21), and God being Israel's true God (44:6). In these passages God paints a picture spanning time from Creation to the consummation of the age. Anna, the Shepherds, the Wise Men, and Mary all looked for the coming day of salvation and redemption. Those present at the birth of Jesus saw that Baby as the start of the culmination process. Simeon sums up best: *"for mine eyes have seen thy salvation"* (Luke 2:30).

Acts 3:19-21 says that from Creation until the *"times of refreshing"* God will deal with man and his spiritual state. Further, the *"times of refreshing"* coincide with the return to the earth of the Lord Jesus Christ. The phrase *"times of refreshing"* can only speak of the Millennial Kingdom foretold by many of the prophets. The previous chapter of this book shows that the Feast of Tabernacles pictures the Millennium. Additionally, all seven feasts picture the spiritual development of a man from salvation to ultimate fellowship with God for eternity in the next age, the New Heavens and the New Earth. A strong parallel exists between Acts 3 and the Feasts. Leviticus 23:3 brings the two together by introducing the idea of Creation as a part of the feast instructions. The connection continues all the way to the final feast, the Feast of Tabernacles.

The Leviticus 23:3 puzzle piece has an unusual shape with the Feasts on one edge and a pattern of labor and rest going back to Creation on the other. It appears to fit another piece, the mysterious eighth day of the Feast of Tabernacles. Once we establish its relationship to the second piece, the third piece, *"the Sabbath of rest,"* will complete the puzzle.

The Second Puzzle Piece: The Eighth Day of Tabernacles

Students of the Feasts have long debated an apparent conflict within the Bible that seems to defy easy resolution:

> *Speak unto the children of Israel, saying the fifteenth day of this seventh month shall be the feast of tabernacles for **seven days** unto the* Lord. . . . ***Seven days** ye shall offering made by fire unto the Lord: on the **eighth day** shall be a holy convocation . . . Also in the fifteenth day of the seventh month . . . ye shall keep a feast unto the*

Lord **seven days**: on the first day shall be a sabbath, and on the **eighth** day shall be a sabbath.

Leviticus 23:34, 36, 39

How can the Lord specially speak of a seven-day (Leviticus 23:34) observance "*unto the LORD*" and then "add" an eighth day? How can the eighth day, a final Sabbath (*shabbaton*), be part of the seven-day Feast of Tabernacles? If the eighth day is actually a separate event closely linked to the Feast of Tabernacles, then the problem is solved. After all, the Feast of Unleavened Bread and the Feast of First Fruits are distinct events and yet share part of the same period of time.

Since the Feast of Tabernacles pictures the Millennium, we must look for an event with a similar theme to associate with the eighth day. The Feast of Trumpets (the first day of Seventh Month) signals the beginning of the Tribulation period. The Day of Atonement (the tenth day of the Seventh Month) signals the return of the Lord to the earth. The Feast of Tabernacles (the fifteenth through the twenty-first day of the Seventh Month) signals the millennial peace of the Messiah's reign. The only remaining event is the consummation of the current age and the beginning of the new age, the New Heavens and the New Earth (2 Peter 3:9-13). The eighth day of Leviticus 23:39 could easily symbolize this connected but distinct event.

The opening Sabbath of the Feast of Tabernacles (Leviticus 23:39) beautifully pictures the unprecedented time of peace and calm for the earth and its inhabitants known as the Millennium. Yet Revelation 20:1-3 speaks of a final rebellion upon the earth at the end of the thousand-year period. Even the Millennium contains rebellion, for sin has not yet been completely banished from the earth. Only in the New Heavens and New Earth does peace truly reign. Thus, the second Sabbath (Leviticus 23:39) pictures the total peace that will come with the New Heavens and the New Earth.

Since the eighth day pictures ultimate peace and a new Creation, it has no connection to the agricultural aspect of the Feasts. While the Feasts are not primarily agricultural celebrations, they nevertheless contain agricultural elements. The absence of an agricultural element in the eighth day explain why it is not mentioned in the instructions for the Feast of Tabernacles given in Deuteronomy 16 since this passage addresses only the agricultural aspect of the feast.

The eighth day symbolizes the culmination of all of God's plans for the present age. Keil calls the eighth day the "solemn close of the whole circle of yearly feasts, and therefore was appended to the close of the last of these feasts as the eighth day of the feast itself" (*Pentateuch* 447). Kellogg also sees it as the finale. The eighth day *shabbaton* is "not a part of the feast of tabernacles merely, but as celebrating the termination of the whole series of sabbatic times from the first to the seventh month" (468). Andrew Bonar calls verse 36 an "annunciation" like Revelation 10:7: "'In the days of the seventh angel . . . the mystery of God shall be finished' -thus raising high our expectations of it, ere it is itself formally declared" (408). Rabbi Donin sees this day, in modern times called Shmini Atzeret, as an independent Feast of Tabernacles (Donin 256). Ancient rabbis called it "a festival by itself" (*Life and Times* 394). While they assign different meanings to the eighth day, all of these men see it as distinct from and yet linked to the Feast of Tabernacles, a Feast of feasts, and a grand climax to all of the Feasts.

Treating the eighth day as symbolic of the Grand Finale seems logical since such an interpretation creates a complete pattern with the first piece, the Creation Sabbath mentioned in Leviticus 23:3. The final and third puzzle piece shows how these two pieces *can* be joined together and are placed in the completed "feast puzzle."

The Third Piece: The Sabbath of Rest

The third puzzle piece is the phrase "*Sabbath of rest.*" The Hebrew expression *shabbat shabbaton* is the intensive form of the word *shabbat,* from which we get our English word Sabbath. In English we would intensify the word Sabbath by adding an adjective (e.g. "ultimate Sabbath") or by altering the word to convey the superlative (i.e. "Sabbathest"). Hebrew achieves the same effect by repeating the word and thereby emphasizing its meaning. *Shabbat shabbaton* is therefore "Sabbath's Sabbath" in English. However, the English Bible translators chose the expression "*Sabbath of rest*" to express the intensified form instead. This expression's rarity in the Bible further intensifies its significance.

The expression "*Sabbath of rest*" occurs only six times in the Bible. Found twice in Exodus, it speaks of the law requiring observance of the seventh-day weekly Sabbath. The remaining four instances occur in Leviticus. Here it appears in connection with the law that requires a Sabbath on the Day of Atonement (Leviticus 16:31; 23:32) and on the Jubilee (Leviticus 25:4). The fourth instance appears in the difficult Leviticus 23:3 passage. The Bible employs this phrase in just two contexts: the Feasts and the six days of work followed by one day of rest pattern.

Before we can understand this phrase's intensified use and the way in which it relates to the Feasts, we must first examine its non-intensified use, Sabbath, which occurs 116 times in the Bible. The root word of Sabbath (*shabbot*) is *shabat,* meaning to "cease," "desist," and "rest" (*BDB* 991; *TWOT* 902). As we might expect, this word makes its first appearance in Genesis 2:2.

And on the seventh day God ended his work which he had made; and he rested [shabat] on the seventh day from all His work which He had made. And God blessed the seventh day and sanctified it: . . .

Genesis 2:2-3

God uniquely sanctifies or sets apart the seventh day and uses it to picture the day on which He "*rested*" or, even better, on which He "ended His creation." The Hebrew word for Sabbath means "completion," "end of a project," or "the finish." Literally it means to "bring to an end" (*TWOT* 902) as Genesis 8:22 shows:

While the earth remaineth, seedtime and harvest, and cold and heat, and summer and winter, and day and night shall not cease [shabat].

Further examples include Jeremiah 31:36 which states that future Israel shall never cease from being a nation and Job 32:1 where we learn that Job's three counselors "ceased" to answer Job because of his righteousness. God's six days of labor followed by a day of ceasing from labor established the pattern. "The pattern is here set for man to follow" (*New Bible Dictionary* 1042). The method that God used to create this pattern reveals its importance.

In Genesis 2:2 the Scriptures record that after six days of creative effort God brought His work to an end or completion. Although many say that God allowed the Creation to evolve over billions of years, the Hebrew text of Genesis 1 does not allow for anything other than a literal, six-day period (see *The Genesis Flood* by Dr. John C. Whitcomb for a full discussion of this subject). In all of the debate about the various evolutionary and creationist theories, we have missed a far more significant question: Why did God take six days to create everything? After all, God could have created it all in an instant.

The only satisfactory answer is that God intentionally **extended** the creation period to six days in order to teach a lesson. Some see the establishment of the six days of labor followed by one of rest pattern as a means to help man in his daily life. However, such an interpretation centers upon **man** rather than God, a clearly faulty theological perspective. All things exist for God's glory and purposes. Those who teach this pattern base it upon the word "*rest*." They see rest as being a time of ease and restoration after labor. If the term "*rest*" had no greater significance, then it would be more appropriate to place the command to observe the Sabbath in the portion of the Law concerned with man's work and not in Leviticus 23, the instructions for the Feasts.

The key to understanding lies in the fundamental meaning of Sabbath, "an ending or bringing to an end." Having completed Creation, God brought His creative work to an end or completion. The seventh day memorializes the completion of God's purpose of Creation. Certainly, it does not memorialize or teach that God was tired and required rest after His work.

Some years ago, when I was visiting England, I went to the town of Tamworth and was escorted on a tour by a seventy-two year old man. After we toured for four or five hours, I was fatigued. I thought that I could not walk any further. My elderly friend then suggested a walk up the hill to a castle. After the fatigues of the day, I drove home and took a rest. I was tired to say the least. I later learned that my host went home and spent several hours gardening! He may not have needed rest, but I certainly did. Unlike man, however, God is never tired or weary.

Hast thou not known? Hast thou not heard, that the everlasting God, the LORD, the Creator of the ends of the earth, fainteth not, neither is weary? There is no searching of his wisdom.

Isaiah 40:28

Adding to the evidence that the Sabbath of Creation and the Leviticus 23:3 Sabbath are connected is the fact that God gave the regular weekly Sabbath as an intentional sign to the nation of Israel.

*Wherefore the children of Israel shall keep the sabbath, to observe the sabbath throughout their generations, for a perpetual covenant. It is a sign between me and **the children of Israel** for ever: for in six days the LORD made heaven and earth, and on the seventh day he rested [ceased] and was refreshed.*

Exodus 31:16-17

The Sabbath and Creation are now linked with the nation of Israel just as the Feasts are. While the link does not yet bring the picture into sharp focus, it clearly demonstrates that something complex is going on between Israel, the Feasts, Creation, and the idea of Sabbath ceasing.

Unfortunately, just after we banished the idea that God needed rest after the effort of creating, we encounter another term suggesting the reverse. God says that He was "*refreshed*" on the seventh day. In reality, however, no real problem exists. The Hebrew term for "*refreshed*," *napash*, means "to be satisfied," much like the sigh of contentment that follows the completion of a complex task (*BDB* 661; *TWOT* 587). Like the artist who after completing a beautiful painting steps back and feels satisfied with the quality of his work, God looked upon His creative work and was satisfied, for "*it was good.*"

God speaks through the weekly Sabbath to show man that the original created universe was beautiful and was precisely the way that He wanted it to be. There was no sin, and the earth was in total harmony with all of Creation. Man existed to glorify God and enjoy Him forever in a perfect universe. After God fulfilled His purpose of Creation, He ceased from creating and savored its existence.

However, sin entered this perfect world and so necessitated God's process of redemption, reconciliation, and restoration back to the perfect (Edenic) state. Over and over, history shows that man will destroy God's creation through his rebellion. The only solution to the problem lay in God's offering salvation by sending His own Son into the world to redeem man. His Son became the substitute Lamb and died at Passover. Through His death and resurrection, Jesus Christ brought full reconciliation. His rising from the dead demonstrated that the wages of sin were paid and that God's justice was satisfied. The means now existed for a restoration to the Edenic state.

One day He will return to rule and reign upon a restored earth as the King of kings. At the present moment, we live between the days of Jesus Christ's resurrection (pictured in the Feast of First Fruits) and the day of His return (the Day of Atonement) and Millennial Kingdom (the Feast of Tabernacles). God gives the Sabbath as a message to Israel and to mankind. To Israel the message says, "God is not done. You are in the 'six days,' but the 'seventh of rest' is coming." To the Church it explains that God's plan is not yet complete. The earth is still suffering from Adam's sin and requires restoration to the Edenic state: *"For we know that the whole creation groaneth and travaileth in pain together until now"* (Romans 8:22). There is a day coming when the earth and heavens will be restored to their original state, the one in which God felt *"refreshed."* The weekly Sabbath pictures God's promise of a coming restoration and reassures us that God's plan still marches on.

God's Plan of the Ages				
First Fruits	**Present 21st Century**	**Day of Atonement**	**Feast of Tabernacles**	**Jubilee**
Christ's Resurrection		**Christ's Return**	**Millennium**	**Sabbath Rest for earth**

Figure 21 – God's Plan of the Ages

God uses the intensive form of the word "Sabbath" to proclaim His promise in a special way. Since the Millennium is primarily an event for national Israel, with the Church ruling and reigning with Christ, the Sabbath is also a proper sign for the conclusion of the Millennial

Kingdom. God first uses the intensive form in His instructions to Israel recorded in Exodus 16:23:

And he said unto them, This is that which the LORD hath said, To morrow is the rest [shabbaton] of the holy sabbath [shabbat] unto the LORD: bake that which ye will bake to day, and seethe that ye will seethe; and that which remaineth over lay up for you to be kept until the morning.

Exodus 16:23

These instructions promised the Israelites that God would provide sufficient manna for the weekly Sabbath. The verse stresses that during the *"rest of the holy Sabbath,"* absolutely no work is allowed. God's curse (Genesis 3:19) brought the "struggle" into work; the Sabbath would have no such struggle. Through the Sabbath, Israel would learn that God would provide all that they needed for sustenance in eternity and that there would no longer be any "struggle" caused by the curse.

The intensive form, *"Sabbath of rest,"* emphasizes that when the ultimate Sabbath comes, there will be a ceasing from all struggles, sin, and labor. The Feasts picture the progress of man toward that end. For national Israel the process begins with the final atonement or cleansing of the nation on the Day of Atonement at the Lord's return to the earth. Thus, the Day of Atonement is the beginning of the *"Sabbath of rest."*

For on that day shall the priest make an atonement for you, to cleanse you, that ye may be clean from all your sins before the LORD. It shall be a sabbath of rest unto you and ye shall humble your souls, by a statute forever.

Leviticus 16:30-31

The Feasts mark each step that leads toward achieving this final cleansing and peace. In a similar manner, God reminds Israel of His promise as He begins the instructions for the Feasts in Leviticus 23:3. The *"Sabbath of rest"* is THE ULTIMATE REST from our labor of striving against sin and its consequences. Such an event is worthy of the intensified Sabbath.

The pieces now seem to fit together. The final confirmation that the pieces do indeed fit the puzzle of the Feasts lies in the presence of "*Sabbath of rest*" in Leviticus 25, the passage that describes the Jubilee.

The Jubilee: The Grand Finale

Recalling that the definition of Sabbath is "the bringing to an end" or "finale," we see that the seventh day of the week brings the work week to an end. People all over the world observe the seven-day pattern. The Seventh Month of the Hebrew year brought the festal observances to an end. The "*Sabbath of rest,*" will bring the present Creation to an end just prior to the creation of the New Heavens and the New Earth. As we move to Leviticus 25, the Jubilee becomes not just another celebration or even another picture. Rather, it becomes **THE** celebration for which all of mankind has waited. The weekly Sabbath is actually just one of several patterns pointing to the Grand Finale or Jubilee.

In Leviticus 23:32 God establishes a "*Sabbath of rest*" for the Day of Atonement. It too illustrates a "bringing to an end" of a previous "journey," man's need for cleansing from his sins. In the case of national Israel, it offers the cleansing that nations also need.

In a small way, I can understand this need. I had a Dachshund named Pretzel who loved to go for walks. Every day he expected a walk around the neighborhood. However, on the rainy days, I avoid looking at him. He would look up and plead to go for a walk. With legs that are only four inches long, however, his belly got very wet and dirty.

If I yield to his wishes on a wet day and took him for a walk, I always regretted it. No matter how I tried to stay clean myself, I got muck all over my shirt when I clean him off at the end of the walk. We are like Pretzel: we are unclean people. Isaiah and Paul both write of this uncleanness:

> *But we are all as an unclean thing, and all our righteousnesses are as filthy rags; and we all do fade as a leaf; and our iniquities, like the wind, have taken us away.*
>
> Isaiah 64:6

There is none righteous, no, not one: there is none that understandeth, there is none that seeketh after God.

Romans 3:10-11

Because God is holy and without sin, He is clean and righteous. There is no way a pure God can associate with us in our sinful state. We are just like Pretzel. God loves us and wants us to enjoy Him forever, but our sin interferes. God cannot be tarnished or stained by our sin. When Jesus Christ died on the tree of Calvary, He paid for our sins and removed their stain. However, each individual must accept that payment and ask that it be applied to himself. John wrote, *"If we confess our sins, He is faithful and just to forgive us our sins and to cleanse us from all unrighteousness"* (1 John 1:9). The shedding of Christ's blood made such cleansing possible. *"But if we walk in the light, as He is in the light, we have fellowship one with another, and the blood of Jesus Christ His Son cleanseth us from all sin"* (1 John 1:7).

Just as individuals need this cleansing, so too does national Israel. The national cleansing is also made possible by the atonement of Jesus Christ. On a future Day of Atonement, Jesus Christ will return to this earth and cleanse Israel from its national sins.

And He shall make an atonement for the holy place, because of the uncleanness of the children of Israel and because of the transgression in all their sins: and so shall He do for the tabernacle of the congregation, that remaineth among them in the midst of their uncleanness.

Leviticus 16:16

One future Day of Atonement, just as the *"Sabbath of rest"* pictures, God will bring an end to Israel's need for a national cleansing of its sin of rejecting the Messiah. Then, God will restore the kingdom, and Jesus Christ will reign in Jerusalem as King of kings and Lord of lords. Israel's struggle, reaching a peak during the Great Tribulation, will finally come to an end (Ezekiel 37-47). But God is not finished!

In the book of Leviticus, God also specifies a year *"Sabbath of rest."*

> *Six years thou shalt sow thy field, and six years thou shalt prune thy*
> *vineyard, and gather in the fruit thereof; but in the seventh year*
> *shall be a Sabbath of rest unto the land, a Sabbath for the LORD;*
> *thou shalt neither sow thy field, nor prune thy vineyard.*
>
> Leviticus 25:3-4

This "*Sabbath of rest*" focuses on the land's needs, not necessarily man's. No one may work the fields during this year. The land lies fallow and "catches its breath" prior to the next harvest. Man must depend upon the LORD to provide a sufficient harvest during the previous year to last until the harvest **after** the Sabbatical year. This "*Sabbath of rest*" reminded the people of Israel that God owned the land. The "land Sabbath" pictures the coming restoration of the earth when God will make the New Heavens and the New Earth (Revelation 21:1).

Therefore, just as God promises a cleansing for Israel in the Seventh Month "*Sabbath of rest*," so too He promises a cleansing rest for the land resulting in the restoration of an Edenic world. But God is still not finished!

The pattern continues. After six days of work followed by one of rest, each week of the year, God brings six months of harvest followed by a period of rest each year. After six years of planting and harvesting, God brings a year of rest. Finally, after *seven* Sabbatical years, God brings the Jubilee.

> *And thou shalt number seven sabbaths of years unto thee, . . . then*
> *thou shalt cause the trumpet of the jubilee to sound on the tenth*
> *day of the seventh month, in the day of atonement shall ye make*
> *the trumpet sound throughout the land. And ye shall hallow the*
> *fiftieth year, and proclaim liberty throughout all the land . . . In*
> *the year of jubilee; ye shall return every man unto his possession.*
>
> Leviticus 25:8-13

For this special period of rest, both the land and the farmer must rest for **two** years, first the Sabbatical year and then the Jubilee year. The farmer must trust the LORD to provide nearly **three** years' worth of food. The Jubilee is a time of total dependence upon God. Furthermore, it is the time when men who have been forced to sell their land automatically regain it and once again possess it, a clear picture of the return to Eden. God declares the land His (Leviticus 25:23) just as it was at Creation.

On the Jubilee slaves are released and captives are freed (Leviticus 25:41). The Scriptures equate this release with the release of Israel from Egypt on the Passover (Leviticus 25:42). God concludes His instructions for the Jubilee by reminding Israel that

> *For unto me the children of Israel are servants: they are my servants whom I brought forth out of the land of Egypt: I am the* Lord *your God.*
>
> Leviticus 25:55

The Jubilee pictures the final, complete restoration of the earth and the heavens to the state that they were in at the beginning when God rested and was refreshed. With this final rest, God is at last finished:

> *And I saw a new heaven and new earth: for the first heaven and the first earth were passed away; and there was no more sea . . . And God shall wipe away all tears from their eyes; and there shall be no more death, neither sorrow, nor crying, neither shall there b any more pain: for the former things are passed away. And he that sat upon the throne said, Behold I make all things new, and he said unto me, Write: for these words are true and faithful. And he said unto me,* **It is done**, *I am Alpha and Omega, the beginning and the end. I will give unto him that is athirst of the fountain of the water of life freely. He that overcometh shall inherit all things; and I will be his God and he shall be my son.*
>
> Revelation 21:1,4-8

Like the booths that the pilgrims of the Feast of Tabernacles burned on the eighth day of the feast, the present heavens and earth will burn at the conclusion of the Millennial Kingdom. The time of transience in the Wilderness of human experience will be over. The New Heavens and the New Earth will replace the old and will be as the old once were.

But the day of the Lord will come as a thief in the night; in which the heavens shall pass away with a great noise, and the elements shall melt with fervent heat, the earth also and the works that are therein shall be burned up. . . . Nevertheless we, according to his promise, look for new heavens and a new earth, wherein dwelleth righteousness.

2 Peter 3:10, 13

God planned history from Creation to the Grand Finale. God will bring all things to the end. The puzzle will become clear to all men. As the first age ends, a new and beautiful one begins. God uses the nation of Israel as His microcosm of history. Each feast pictures elements of that journey, not just for Israel but also for each one of us. If we accept God's path, it will lead to the Jubilee and the New Heavens and the New Earth. Like Adam, we too can walk and talk with God throughout eternity because God makes it possible. If we receive His free gift of eternal life by accepting the Lord Jesus Christ's sacrifice upon the Cross to pay for our sins, and if we ask Him to be our Savior, all of these future events await us, not for our glory but for His. For we are created for His good pleasure and will. Unfortunately, the very same passage that tells us of the New Heavens and the New Earth also speaks of judgment for those who reject the Lord Jesus Christ:

But the fearful and unbelieving, and the abominable, and murderers, and whoremongers, and sorcerers, and idolaters, and all liars, shall have their part in the lake which burneth with fire and brimstone, which is the second death.

Revelation 21:8

Each one must decide which fork in the path of life he will take. One leads to eternal rest with God while the other leads to an eternal death separated from God.

The Feasts picture not just the history of a nation, not just the spiritual journey of a man, but also the span of history from Genesis 1:1 to Revelation 21:1. With the conclusion of the Feasts, man has the whole picture. Eternity waits, and Revelation 21 gives each of us a glimpse of things yet to come. We praise God that in His condescension to man, He gave such a beautiful picture through the Feasts of the LORD. Will you be at the ultimate appointment with God in eternity?

The "*Sabbath of rest*" is the End of the Beginning

BIBLIOGRAPHY

Alford, Henry. The Greek Testament: A Critical and Exegetical Commentary. 4 vols. Chicago: Moody, 1958.

Albright, W. F. "The Gezer Calendar." *Bulletin of the American School of Oriental Research* 92 (1943):22-23.

Barclay, William. *The Gospel of John*. Vol. 1. Philadelphia: Westminster, 1958.

Berkhof, Louis. *Systematic Theology*. 4th ed. Grand Rapids: Eerdmans, 1941.

Bloch, Abraham P. The Biblical and Historical Background of the Jewish Holy Days. New York: KTAV, 1978.

Bonar, Andrew. *A Commentary on the Book of Leviticus*. N.p.: James Nisbet, 1852. Grand Rapids: Baker, 1978.

Bromiley, Geoffrey W. Theological Dictionary of the New Testament - Abridged in One Volume. Grand Rapids: Eerdmans, 1985.

Brown, Francis, S. R. Driver, and Charles A. Briggs eds. *Hebrew and English Lexicon of the Old Testament*. Oxford: Clarendon, 1978.

Brasch, R. The Judaic Heritage: Its Teachings, Philosophy and Symbols. New York: David McKay, 1969.

Buksbazen, Victor. *The Gospel In The Feasts of Israel*. Fort Washington, Pennsylvania: Christian Literature Crusade, 1954.

Bush, George. Notes, Critical and Practical on the Book of Leviticus. New York: Mark H. Newman, 1850.

Chafer, Lewis Sperry. *Systematic Theology*. Ed. John F. Walvoord. Wheaton, Illinois: Victor, 1988.

Congdon, Robert R. "The Feast of Trumpets: A Memorial." Diss. Grace Theological Seminary, 1981.

Davies, G. Henton. "Memorial, Memory." *The Interpreter's Dictionary of the Bible*. Ed. G. A. Buttrick. Nashville: Abingdon, 1962.

Davis, John J. *Biblical Numerology.* Winona Lake, Indiana: BMH, 1968.

---. Moses and the Gods of Egypt: Studies in Exodus. Winona Lake, Indiana: BMH, 1986.

Delitzsch, F. *Commentary on the Old Testament in Ten Volumes: Job.* Vol. 4. Fifth reprint ed. Grand Rapids: Eerdmans, 1978.

---. Commentary on the Old Testament in Ten Volumes: Psalms. Vol. 5. Fifth reprint ed. Grand Rapids: Eerdmans, 1978.

Donin, Hayim Halevy. To Be a Jew: A Guide to Jewish Observance in Contemporary Life. N.p.: Basic Books, 1991.

Edersheim, Alfred. The Life and Times of Jesus the Messiah. N.p.: MacDonald, n.d.

---. The Temple: Its Ministry and Services as They Were at the Time of Jesus Christ. Reprint ed. Grand Rapids: Eerdmans, 1978.

Elliger, K. et al., eds. *Biblia Hebraica Stuttgartensia.* Stuttgart: Deutsche Bibelstiftung, 1977. "Calendar." *Encyclopedia Americana.* New York: Americana Corporation, 1964 edition.

Fensham, F. C. "Covenant, Alliance." *New Bible Dictionary.* 2nd ed. Ed. J. D. Douglas. Wheaton, Illinois: Tyndale, 1962.

Freeman, D. "Feasts." *New Bible Dictionary.* 2nd ed. Ed. J. D. Douglas. Wheaton, Illinois: Tyndale, 1962.

Freeman, Hobart E. "Festivals." *Wycliffe Bible Encyclopedia.* Ed. Charles F. Pfeiffer, Howard F. Vos, and John Rhea. Chicago: Moody, 1975.

French, Ivan H. "Outline Studies in the Life of Christ." Syllabus. Winona Lake, Indiana: Grace Theological Seminary, n.d.

Funderburk, Guy B. "Calendar." *The Zondervan Pictorial Bible Dictionary.* Ed. Merrill C. Tenney. Grand Rapids: Zondervan, 1977.

Gaster, Theodor H. *Festivals of the Jewish Year.* New York: Morrow, 1953.

Gill, John. "An Exposition of the Old and New Testament in Nine Volumes." Ed. Larry Pierce. *Online Bible 6.3.* CD-ROM. Bronson, Missouri: Online Bible USA, 1996.

Gower, Ralph. New Manners and Customs of Bible Times. Chicago: Moody, 1987.

Greenstone, Julius H. *Jewish Feasts and Fasts.* Philadelphia: Jewish Publication Society, 1945.

Harris, R. Laird, Gleason L. Archer, Jr., and Bruce K. Waltke, eds. *Theological Wordbook of the Old Testament.* 2 vols. Chicago: Moody, 1980.

Harrison, R. K. *Introduction to the Old Testament.* Grand Rapids: Eerdmans, 1969.

---. "Leviticus an Introduction and Commentary." *Tyndale Old Testament Commentaries.* Vol. 3. Ed. Donald J. Wiseman. Downers Grove, Illinois: InterVarsity, 1980.

Hoehner, Harold W. "Pentecost." *Wycliffe Bible Encyclopedia.* Ed. Charles F. Pfeiffer,

Howard F. Vos, and John Rhea. Chicago: Moody, 1975.

Jacobs, Louis. "Rosh Hashanah." *Encyclopedia Judaica.* Jerusalem: Keter, 1971.

Josephus. *The Works of Josephus: Complete and Unabridged.* Trans. William Whiston. Peabody, Massachusetts: Hendrickson, 1987.

JPS Torah Commentary: Leviticus. Philadelphia: Jewish Publication Society, 1989.

Kaiser, Walter C., Jr. *Toward an Old Testament Theology.* Grand Rapids: Zondervan, 1978.

Keil, C. F. *Commentary on the Old Testament in Ten Volumes: Chronicles.* Vol. 3. Fifth reprint ed. Grand Rapids: Eerdmans, 1978.

---. *Commentary on the Old Testament in Ten Volumes: Ezra.* Vol. 3. Fifth reprint ed. Grand Rapids: Eerdmans, 1978.

---. Commentary on the Old Testament in Ten Volumes: Nehemiah. Vol. 3. Fifth reprint ed. Grand Rapids: Eerdmans, 1978.

---. Commentary on the Old Testament in Ten Volumes: Pentateuch. Vol. 1. Fifth reprint ed. Grand Rapids: Eerdmans, 1978.

Kellogg, S. H. *The Book of Leviticus: The Expositor's Bible.* Ed. W. Robertson Nicoll. New York: Armstrong, 1891.

Kent, Homer A. *The Epistle to the Hebrews.* Winona Lake, Indiana: BMH, 1972.

Kidner, Derek. "Genesis: An Introduction and Commentary." *Tyndale Old Testament Commentaries.* Vol. 1. Ed. Donald J. Wiseman. Downers Grove, Illinois: InterVarsity, 1967.

---. Psalms: An Introduction and Commentary in 2 Volumes. Downers Grove, Illinois: InterVarsity, 1975.

Knoebel, Peter S. *Gates of the Seasons: A Guide to the Jewish Year.* New York: Central Conference of American Rabbis, 1983.

Lange, John Peter. Commentary on the Holy Scriptures, Critical, Doctrinal, and Homiletical: Leviticus. Trans. Philip Schaff. Grand Rapids: Zondervan, n.d.

Larson, Gary N. "The Nature and Development of the Jewish Calendar." Diss. Wheaton College, 1982.

Marshall, I. Howard. "The Acts of the Apostles: An Introduction and Commentary." *The Tyndale New Testament Commentary.* Vol. 5. Ed. R. V. G. Tasker. Grand Rapids: Eerdmans, 1980.

Martin, W. J. "Bread." *New Bible Dictionary.* 2nd ed. Ed. J. D. Douglas. Wheaton, Illinois: Tyndale, 1962.

McClain, Alva J. *Daniel's Prophecy of the 70 Weeks.* Grand Rapids: Zondervan, 1969.

---. The Greatness of the Kingdom: An Inductive Study of the Kingdom of God. Winona Lake, Indiana: BMH, 1974.

McClain, Alva J. and Charles R. Smith. "Christian Theology: Salvation and the Christian Life." Syllabus. Winona Lake, Indiana: Grace Theological Seminary, 1978.

McClain, Alva J. and John C. Whitcomb. "Christian Theology: Dispensational Eschatology." Syllabus. Winona Lake, Indiana: Grace Theological Seminary, n.d.

McQuaid, Elwood. "Come September." *Israel My Glory* Aug.-Sept. 1994: 4.

---. *The Outpouring.* Bellmawr, New Jersey: The Friends of Israel Gospel Ministry: 1990.

Moorehead, W. *G. Studies in the Mosaic Institutions.* 3rd ed. Dayton: United Brethren, 1909.

Morgenstern, Julian. "Three Calendars of Ancient Israel." *Hebrew Union College Annual* (1925):72-82.

Morris, Leon. *The Apostolic Preaching of the Cross.* 3rd ed. Grand Rapids: Eerdmans, 1965.

---. *The Atonement: Its Meaning and Significance.* Downers Grove, Illinois: InterVarsity, 1983.

Murray, John. *The Collected Writings of John Murray.* 2 vols. Carlisle, Pennsylvania: Banner of Truth, 1977.

Markowitz, William. "Calendar." *New Grolier Multimedia Encyclopedia.* Release 6. CD-ROM. N.p.: Online Computer Systems, 1993.

Pentecost, J. Dwight. *Things to Come: A Study in Biblical Eschatology.* Grand Rapids: Zondervan, 1964.

Perowne, J. J. Stewart. *The Book of Psalms.* 2 vols. Andober, England: Warren F. Draper, 1876.

Pierce, Larry. *Online Bible 6.3.* CD-ROM. Bronson, Missouri: Online Bible USA, 1996.

Pink, Arthur W. *Gleanings in the Godhead.* Chicago: Moody, 1975.

Pritchard, James B., ed. *The Ancient Near East.* Vol. 1. Princeton: Princeton UP, 1975.

Rhea, John. "The Time of the Oppression and the Exodus." *Grace Journal* 2.1 (Winter 1961): 7ff.

---. "Exodus." *Wycliffe Bible Encyclopedia.* Charles F. Pfeiffer, Howard F. Vos, and John Rhea, eds. Chicago: Moody, 1975.

Robertson, A. T. *Word Pictures in the New Testament.* 6 vols. New York: Harpers, 1930.

Rodgers, Thomas R. *Hebrews.* Newburgh, Indiana: Impact, 1990.

---. *The Panorama of the Old Testament.* Newburgh, Indiana: Impact, 1988.

Ryrie, Charles C. *Basic Theology.* Winona Lake, Indiana: BMH, 1986.

Saggs, H. W. F. *The Greatness That Was Babylon.* New York: Hawthorn; New York: Mentor, 1962.

Schultz, Samuel J. "Leviticus: God Among His People." *Everyman's Bible Commentary.* Chicago: Moody, 1983.

Segal, J. B. "The Hebrew Festivals and the Calendar." *Journal of Semantic Studies* 6 (1963).

Shepherd, Coulson. Jewish Holy Days: Their Prophetic and Christian Significance. Neptune, New Jersey: Loizeaux, 1961.

Showers, Renald. Maranatha - Our Lord Come!: A Definitive Study of the Rapture of the Church. Bellmawr, New Jersey: Friends of Israel, 1995.

Singer, Isidore, ed. *Jewish Encyclopedia.* New York: Funk and Wagnalls, 1905.

Smick, Elmer B. "Calendar." *Wycliffe Bible Encyclopedia.* Ed. Charles F. Pfeiffer, Howard F. Vos, and John Rhea. Chicago: Moody, 1975.

Snaith, Norman H., ed. *The Century Bible: Leviticus and Numbers.* N.p.: Nelson, 1967.

Spurgeon, C. H. *The Treasury of David.* 2 vols. Nashville: Nelson, n.d.

Strong, James. *Strong's Exhaustive Concordance.* Gordonsville, Tennessee: Dugan, n.d.

Strauss, Lehman. *God's Prophetic Calendar.* Neptune, New Jersey: Loizeaux, 1987.

Thayer, Joseph Henry. *Greek-English Lexicon of the New Testament.* Grand Rapids: Zondervan, 1977.

Unger, Merrill F. *Unger's Bible Dictionary.* 3rd ed. Chicago: Moody, 1960.

Unger, Merrill F. and William White, eds. Nelson's Expository Dictionary of the Old Testament. Part of Vine's Expository Dictionary of Biblical Words. Nashville: Nelson, 1985.

Vos, Geerhardus. *Biblical Theology: Old and New Testament.* Carlisle, Pennsylvania: Banner of Truth, 1975.

Walvoord, John F. "Israel's Blindness." *Bibliotheca Sacra* 102 (July 1945). *Webster's New World Dictionary.* Ed. David B. Buralnik. New York: World, 1959.

Wenham, Gordon J. *The Book of Leviticus.* Grand Rapids: Eerdmans, 1979.

Wiersbe, Warren W. *Be God's Guest: Feasts of Leviticus 23.* Lincoln, Nebraska: Back to the Bible, 1982.

Wolf, Herbert. *Haggai and Malachi.* Chicago: Moody, 1976.

Wood, Leon. *A Survey of Israel's History.* Grand Rapids: Zondervan, 1970.

Supplementary Readings

Bamberger, Bernard Jacob. *The Torah: A Modern Commentary--Leviticus.* New York: Union of American Hebrew Congregations, 1979.

Birnbaum, Philip. *A Book of Jewish Concepts.* New York: Hebrew Publishing, 1964.

Childs, Brevard S. The Book of Exodus: A Critical Theological Commentary. Philadelphia: Westminster, 1974.

Edidin, Ben. *Jewish Holidays and Festivals.* New York: Jordan, 1940.

Ellecott, C. J. *A Bible Commentary.* Vol. 1, New York: Cassell, 1906.

Gesenius, William. *Hebrew and English Lexicon of the Old Testament.* Boston: Crocker and Brewster, 1849.

Goodman, Philip. *The Rosh Hashanah Anthology.* Philadelphia: Jewish Publication Society, 1970.

Gray, George Buchanan. A Critical and Exegetical Commentary on Numbers. New York: Scribner, 1920.

Green, William Scott, ed. *Approaches to Ancient Judaism: Theory and Practice.* Missoula, Montana: Scholar's Press for Brown University, 1978.

Greenstone, Julius H. *The Holy Scripture with Commentary: Numbers.* Philadelphia: Jewish Publication Society, 1939.

Hastings, James. *A Dictionary of the Bible.* New York: Scribner, 1900.

Jukes, Andrew. *The Law of the Offerings.* Glasgow: Pickering and Inglis, n.d.

Kaiser, Walter C., Jr. *Toward Rediscovering the Old Testament.* Grand Rapids: Zondervan, 1987.

Kraus, Hans-Joachim. *Worship In Israel: A Cultic History of the Old Testament.* Trans. G. Buswell. Richmond, Virginia: John Knox, 1965.

Lockyer, Herbert. *All the Holy Days and Holidays.* Grand Rapids: Zondervan, 1968.

Mackie, G.M. *Bible Manners and Customs.* New York: Revell, 1898.

New Testament and Wycliffe Bible Commentary. New York: Iversen-Norman, 1971.

Noordtzig, A. *Bible Students Commentary: Leviticus.* Grand Rapids: Zondervan, 1982.

Noth, Martin. *Old Testament Library: Leviticus.* Philadelphia: Westminster, 1965.

Orr, James, ed. The International Standard Bible Encyclopedia. Grand Rapids: Eerdmans, 1939.

Ramm, Bernard. *Protestant Biblical Interpretation.* Grand Rapids: Baker, 1970.

Rasmussen, Carl. *Zondervan NIV Atlas of the Bible.* Grand Rapids: Zondervan, 1989.

Rosen, Ceil and Moishe. *Christ in the Passover.* Chicago: Moody, 1978.

---. Share the New Life with a Jew. Chicago: Moody, 1976.

Tan, Paul Lee. *The Interpretation of Prophecy.* Winona Lake, Indiana: BMH, 1974.

The Torah: The Five Books of Moses. Philadelphia: Jewish Publication Society, 1962.

Tenny, Merrill C., ed. *Zondervan Pictorial Encyclopedia of the Bible.* Grand Rapids: Zondervan, 1975.

Vainstein, Yaacov. *The Cycle of the Jewish Year: A Study of the Festivals and of Selections From the Liturgy.* Jerusalem: Department for Torah Education and Culture in the Diaspora/The World Zionist Organization, 1964.

Weingreen, J. A Practical Grammar For Classical Hebrew. Oxford: Clarendon, 1972.

Willmington, Harold L. *Willmington's Survey of the Old Testament.* Wheaton, Illinois: Victor, 1987.

Young, R. *Analytical Concordance to the Bible.* New York: Funk and Wagnalls, n.d.

Scripture Index

The European Union and the *Supra-Religion*: Setting the Stage for the Final Act?

Over 2500 years ago God revealed through the prophet Daniel that the Roman Empire will revive as a world power prior to the return of Jesus Christ to establish His earthly, Millennial Kingdom. Inspired by Satan, this empire will be "diverse" or unique in history, uniting a supra-government with a world-wide supra-religion. In his attempt to thwart Christ's return to claim His kingdom, Satan will use this empire to persecute and nearly destroy Israel, a nation crucial to the program of God.

Dr. Congdon presents a compelling case, demonstrating just how the European Union may in fact be the embryo of the restored Roman Empire. His Bible knowledge and analytical engineering background, coupled with his six-year EU residency, give him a unique perspective on world events and enable him to explore the possibility that the "stage" is being set for the final act of God's revealed plan for history.

Price: $15.99
Paperback: 296 pages
ISBN: 978-1-60266-679-5
Shipping weight: 14.4 ounces

Other Books by Robert R. Congdon

Study Guide: The European Union and the Supra-Religion: Setting the Stage for the Final Act?
        Cat. #7010
The Patterns of God Series: When the Glory Returns
        Cat. #7008
The Patterns of God Series: Understanding the Chronology of the Crucifixion Week
        Cat. #7009

To order these materials or for more information on this subject, this ministry, our free email newsletter, or to contact us, write or email:

Continued on back >

Congdon Ministries International
PO Box 1785
Greer, SC 29652

Orders for material: Orders@InternetBibleInstitute.com

To contact the author: RCongdon@InternetBibleInstitute.com

website: www.Congdon-Ministries.com

Dr. Congdon is available to speak at your church, Bible conference, Pastors' conference, for radio interviews, or other occasions by contacting him at the above address.

9 781615 070725